"Striving to be a true woman of God? This book is a valuable guide."

— ELISABETH ELLIOT,
AUTHOR

"In this most difficult of times for women confronted by a challenging and often hostile culture, Susan Hunt comes forward with precisely the right message. *The True Woman* is a brave book, a demanding book, but at the same time a most encouraging and inspiring book as it directs women into the Scripture-charted path of 'reflecting their redemption.' In sharp contrast to the half-truths spawned by the feminist movement of the past three decades, the language of this book goes to the theological center of all that it means to be a godly woman in today's ungodly world. Every American woman should have the opportunity to read this book."

— DR. D. JAMES KENNEDY,
CORAL RIDGE PRESBYTERIAN
CHURCH

"These reflections on the great themes of life are refreshing for their candor, vigor, and truthfulness; for nothing is more important than to know who we are and how we should live before God."

— DR. DAVID F. WELLS,
GORDON-CONWELL THEOLOGICAL
SEMINARY

"Susan Hunt's concern to offer biblical principles with personal accounts of women living for Christ's glory provides moving and poignant reading. Her ability to show the dignity of those who love to live for God gives us a vision of the glory heaven intends for women."

— PRESIDENT BRYAN CHAPELL,
COVENANT THEOLOGICAL
SEMINARY

THE TRUE WOMAN

CROSSWAY BOOKS
BY SUSAN HUNT

Spiritual Mothering
The True Woman

THE TRUE WOMAN

*The Beauty and Strength
of a Godly Woman*

Susan Hunt

Prepared for
Women In the Church

CE&P

Presbyterian Church in America
CHRISTIAN EDUCATION AND PUBLICATIONS
1852 Century Place, Suite 101, Atlanta, GA 30345

CROSSWAY BOOKS • WHEATON, ILLINOIS
A DIVISION OF GOOD NEWS PUBLISHERS

For Leader's Guide
Call 1-800-283-1357

The True Woman

Copyright © 1997 by Susan Hunt

Published by Crossway Books
   a division of Good News Publishers
   1300 Crescent Street
   Wheaton, Illinois 60187

Cover design: Cindy Kiple

First printing, 1997

Printed in the United States of America

ISBN 0-89107-927-0

Scripture references designated (NKJV) are taken from the *New King James Version*. Copyright © 1982, Thomas Nelson, Inc., Publishers. Used by permission.

Unless otherwise marked, Scripture is taken from *The Holy Bible: New International Version*®. Copyright © 1973, 1978, 1984 by International Bible Society. Used by permission of Zondervan Publishing House. All rights reserved.

  The "NIV" and "New International Version" trademarks are registered in the United States Patent and Trademark Office by International Bible Society. Use of either trademark requires the permission of International Bible Society.

Library of Congress Cataloging-in-Publication Data
Hunt, Susan, 1940-
  The true woman : the beauty and strength of a godly woman /
Susan Hunt.
    p. cm.
  Includes bibliographical references.
  ISBN 0-89107-927-0
  1. Women—Religious life. 2. Women in the Bible. I. Title.
  BV4527.H86 1997
  248.8'43—DC20   96-36307

05		04		03		02		01		00		99		98		97
15	14	13	12	11	10	9	8	7	6	5	4	3	2	1

DEDICATION

To the true women in my life:

My mother
Mary Kathryn McLaurin
with admiration for her example
as a true woman

Our daughters and daughter-in-love
Kathryn Barriault
Laurin Coley
Shannon Hunt
with gratitude that they are true women

Our granddaughters
Mary Kathryn Barriault
Susan McLaurin Barriault
Cassie McLaurin Coley
with the prayer that they will be true women

And in memory of my great-grandmother
Cassie Barnes
A true woman who prayed for
the children yet to be born

"The children of your servants will live in your presence;
their descendants will be established before you."
—Psalm 102:28

CONTENTS

ACKNOWLEDGMENTS

This book is a family affair. My family saturates me with their love, support, and prayers. My husband, Gene, read every word, talked me through the rough places, and watched ball games with me when my mind was on overload and needed a break.

Our children cooperated superbly—no one had a baby while I was writing. This was a first! Baby Cassie arrived after the manuscript was turned in, but in time for her name to be on the dedication page. Good timing.

Three of my sisters in Christ made huge investments in this book. Lynn Brookside, Karen Grant, and Barbara Thompson read each chapter as it was written. Their reactions and suggestions strengthened the book and reassured me. These true women are true friends.

My church is a place where believers share their gifts and graces with one another. I am especially blessed by the fellowship of my Sunday school class, the patience of the Tuesday morning women's Bible study as they allow me to teach what I am writing, the prayer support of the men's Wednesday morning prayer group, and the godly leadership of our elders. The Foreword by the elders of my church is more than an endorsement of this book. It is a covering for which I am very thankful.

Thank you to the prayer warriors across the country who faithfully surrounded this project with prayer protection.

My thanks to the Presbyterian Church in America Christian Education staff—especially Charles Dunahoo, Dennis Bennett, and Stacey VanVoorhis—and to the Women's Advisory Subcommittee. I am grateful that I work in the context of their oversight, advice, help, and encouragement.

I am especially grateful for the true women who opened the pages of their lives and allowed us to read what the Lord has done for them. Their stories are their gifts to us, and it is a costly gift. An exorbitant amount of emotional and spiritual energy was required to open and share this portion of their life-diaries, but I am confident that this investment will reap rich rewards in God's kingdom. As you read their stories, I am sure you will join me in praising God for His grace in their lives and in thanking them for touching our lives with that grace.

$\mathscr{F}$OREWORD

"All Scripture is inspired by God and profitable for teaching, for reproof, for correction, and for training in righteousness" (2 Timothy 3:16). So often we each want that inspired Word to say what we want it to say to meet our own specific purpose.

Thankfully, God's Word is His absolute standard regardless of the shifting sands of the times or the conventional wisdom of men. Susan Hunt has quite literally taken God's Word for what it says and seeks to practice that Word in both her personal and professional life.

In *The True Woman* Susan Hunt gives the scriptural basis for the trust, confidence, and sanctuary that the Lord has established for women in the protection that Christ offers through His church and the eldership within that body.

As a body of elders, we endorse, approve, and encourage this book and its wise counsel to modern-day women in their quest for the security and peace that the church of Jesus Christ must offer to those who truly seek Him.

May both the reader and the author of this fine work be blessed.

The Elders
Midway Presbyterian Church (PCA),
Powder Springs, GA

Todd Allen	Larry Judy
Don Barnett	Wes Richardson
Ken Dewhurst	John Ross
David Didier	James Scott
Jim Jacobs	Paul VanNortwick

$\mathcal{I}$NTRODUCTION

I f you have read any of my previous books, you will quickly realize that this book is a different verse of the same song. The same
themes and format are unapologetically present. Each book stands
alone, but the greater value is in the overlay of one upon another.
Each book is hopefully profitable for individual reading, but the
greater value is when a group of women gathers and studies
together. Thus a *Leader's Guide** with clear instructions for interac-
tive studies is available for each book.

So why a new verse to my song of calling women to biblical
womanhood and calling the church to utilize the gifts of women
in kingdom work? In many ways, these books represent my own
personal pilgrimage.

As I grappled with the question of how the church could utilize the full range of the gifts of women without violating male
headship, my friend Peggy Hutcheson and I wrote *Leadership for
Women in the Church*.

Then as I discovered the powerful potential of women nur-

**Leader's Guides may be ordered by calling 1-800-283-1357.*

turing women, I wrote *Spiritual Mothering: The Titus 2 Model for Women Mentoring Women.*

This led to more questions. Was women nurturing women the goal or a means to the goal? What was the nurturance to produce? The answers are in *By Design.*

All of these books have hinted at what woman is to *be*, but primarily they have dealt with what woman is designed to *do*. Perhaps I had to progress to this life stage before I was ready to give reflective thought to *being* rather than *doing*. You can't really separate the two—we *do* what we *be*. But it has been invigorating to ponder the question: What kind of woman does it take to do what we have been designed to do? The answer: A true woman.

Learning what it means to be a true woman is an endeavor that is richer when done with other women, per Titus 2. Themes and precepts mentioned in this book are expanded and applied in the *Leader's Guide* for group study.

Each chapter concludes with a personal reflection section. I encourage you to keep a journal of your thoughts. This discipline will help you process and remember the things discussed in each chapter. If you are doing this in a group study or even with one other woman, you will encourage one another as you share what the Lord is teaching you. This kind of interaction with other women will help you to experience Paul's purpose for the Colossians and my prayer for you:

> *My purpose is that they may be encouraged in heart and united in love, so that they may have the full riches of complete understanding, in order that they may know the mystery of God, namely, Christ, in whom are hidden all the treasures of wisdom and knowledge.*
>
> — *Colossians 2:2-3*

PART ONE

THE TRUE WOMAN
VERSUS
THE NEW WOMAN

What is the true woman?

How did the concept evolve?

How did it dissolve?

Does it need to be rediscovered?

❧

MY PRAYER

That you will be captivated by this concept
and stirred to be a true woman.

❧

MY CHALLENGE

"I urge you, [sisters], in view of God's mercy
to offer your bodies as living sacrifices, holy and
pleasing to God—this is your spiritual act of worship.
Do not conform any longer to the pattern of this world,
but be transformed by the renewing of your mind. Then
you will be able to test and approve what God's will is—
his good, pleasing and perfect will."

— ROMANS 12:1-2

❧

*I*NFERTILITY

Children. I want children. Not just a baby. Not just a child. I want children. Three of them. If I were younger, I might want more, but at thirty-four three seems like a good number. Marrying a little late and moving across the country a couple of times as well as a long-running struggle to pay the rent delayed the real trying for a while. The trying has been going on for a long time now. Not as long as many of you, but much longer than most.

To no avail. No children. Not one pregnancy. I have never experienced that wonder of knowing that there is a life inside of me. Instead, there is a longing that will not be filled, that will not be diminished, that will not end this side of heaven without children to fill it.

Nothing else in my life has been as baffling to me as not being able to conceive a child. My emotions hide even from myself, spilling out in tears of sadness or anger at the most inopportune times. There have been no days of real clarity, no times when a light has come on to show the way—not even a little. But the mysterious and marvelous mercy of God has convinced me of one thing in all of this—it is dark because I am in that deep, hidden place under God's wing.

Certainly, the inability to bear children to the glory of God is due to the sinfulness of sin and its effect on all of life. It is not that God punishes us by not allowing us to give birth to the offspring we most desperately desire. It is rather that we, along with all of creation, suffer the wretched consequences of the sin of our first mother and father, Adam and Eve, compounded by the sin of all the sinners who have come after them. And that, of course, is all of us.

Since this is so, I know that, as with all of life, I must not put my trust in anything other than God, even in the provision of a child. This does not necessarily mean that I may not use medical intervention to try to conceive a child. It does not mean that adoption is not an option to pursue. Rather, I trust that God in His mercy has given us these means as part of His redemption from the effects of the Fall.

At times the knowledge that God has given His covenant of grace to believers and their children makes not being able to have a child even more difficult to understand and bear. God has rescued me from such a desperate place and has given me such a glorious glimpse of Himself that I want, with all that is within me, to see this passed on to the next generation of my family, my children.

My heart cries out, "Why, O God, will You not answer this prayer? Why will You not do this simple thing for me and for Your own name's sake? You do it for so many so easily. You give children to those who will never teach them about Your marvelous grace. Why not to me?" With thoughts like these, it is easy to fall into deep despair, and at times I certainly do. When this happens, God in His time and His various graceful ways, comes to me to remind me that I am not alone.

He does not, as so many do, tell me that "my time will come." He does not say that if I will just relax and not try so hard, everything will be okay. He does not say, "If you adopt a baby, you'll get pregnant." He does say that He is with me. He weeps with me as Jesus wept for Lazarus. He reminds me that He is good and that He can be trusted with my heart. Any doubt of that was wiped away at the Cross.

He has given His best to me, His own beautiful, beloved Child. Will He withhold any good thing from me? No, never. Is Jesus enough to make up for this aching void in my soul? I do not always feel that it is so. But it is. Jesus loves me—this I know.

—Debbie Trickett,
Atlanta, GA

CHAPTER
ONE

ER TIME

To a certain extent, woman is the conservator of her nation's welfare. Her virtue, if firm and uncorrupted, will stand sentinel over that of the empire.

Female Piety

I am thrilled with the plethora of books, tapes, videos, and magazines that are helping Christians think biblically and strategically as we live out our faith in a post-Christian culture. But as I read, listen, and watch, I wonder if a foundational essential for salting culture has been missed. The French philosopher Alexis de Tocqueville discovered this secret ingredient when he traveled through the United States in 1831. He wrote about it in his classic work *Democracy in America*: "No free communities ever existed without morals, and . . . morals are the work of woman. Consequently, whatever affects the condition of women, their habits and their opinions, has great political importance in my eyes."[1]

The nineteenth-century preacher John Angell James was also aware of woman's position as the heart of culture: "The greatest influence on earth, whether for good or for evil, is possessed by woman. Let us study the history of by-gone ages, the state of barbarism and civilization; of the east and the west, of Paganism and Christianity; of antiquity and the middle ages; of the mediaeval and modern times; and we shall find that there is nothing which more decidedly separates them than the condition of woman."[2]

I can almost hear the groans of women. "Where are the men today who place such high value on womanhood?" Some have chosen to land on that question and write books filled with examples of how men have disappointed, discouraged, distressed, degraded, and disgraced women. But that is blame-shifting. The painful reality is that the question is not: "Where are men like Tocqueville and James?" The question is: "Where are the true women who are having such a magnanimous magnetism on our culture?"

THE REAL THING

But what is meant by the term "the true woman"?

The dictionary defines true as "consistent with fact or reality; exactly conforming to a rule, standard, or pattern." Some of the meanings of the Greek words translated true, truly, and truth in the New Testament include unconcealed, actual, true to fact, real, ideal, genuine, sincere, the reality lying at the basis of an appearance, and the manifested veritable essence of a matter.[3]

The true woman is the real thing. She is a genuine, authentic Masterpiece. The Master has set eternity in her heart and is conforming her to His own image. There is consistency in her outward behavior because it is dictated by the reality of her inner life. That reality is her redemption.

The true woman is a reflection of her redemption.

Since the fall of Adam, and until Christ returns, there cannot be a thoroughly true reflection of His image. Sin brings confusion, pandemonium, and death to the soul, and its remnants haunt us even after we are born again. But the radical entrance of grace into the heart brings life, order, and sanity. By the transforming power of the Gospel, the Christian woman is empowered by God's Spirit to give an increasingly true reflection of her Savior and thus to be a true woman.

"True womanhood" was the accepted and expected concept of womanhood in mid-nineteenth-century America. Women's books and magazines cultivated and propagated this concept. According to Barbara Welter, "Authors who addressed themselves to the subject of women in the mid-nineteenth century used this phrase as frequently as writers on religion mentioned God. Neither group felt it necessary to define their favorite terms; they simply assumed—with some justification—that readers would intuitively understand exactly what they meant."[4]

I first read of the true-woman concept in *No Place for Truth*. In this book, David Wells, professor of historical and systematic theology at Gordon-Conwell Theological Seminary, writes:

> Moralists and campaigners in the nineteenth century almost invariably addressed their pleas and admonitions to women, to the hands that rocked the cradles. Men, it seemed, were beyond redemption unless their womenfolk could get to them. Carousing and cavorting were accepted as an inevitable part of being male, but it was felt that if women were in some way to fall as well, the very fabric of society would be rent. For this peculiar role in the world, women were not sequestered away from wickedness, as was often the case in Europe, but . . . were encouraged to develop the strength of mind and independence of thought without which their innocence would soon be overcome.[5]

Various attributes characterized the nineteenth-century true woman. Welter summarizes these into "four cardinal virtues—piety, purity, submissiveness and domesticity."[6] Provocative words to say the least! Part of our task will be to determine if these are biblical virtues. If they are, then we must dismantle our twentieth-century definitions of these words and discover the biblical definitions.

THEN AND NOW

Imagine living in mid-nineteenth-century culture where you would be out of sync if you opposed this standard. Let me jump-start your imaginings by quoting from some books and magazines of that era.

Imagine sitting in your doctor's office scanning your favorite magazine, *The Lady at Home*, and reading: ". . . even if we cannot reform the world in a moment, we can begin the work by reforming ourselves and our households—It is woman's mission. Let her not look away from her own little family circle for the means of producing moral and social reforms, but begin at home."[7]

Imagine sitting by the fire with a cup of tea and a new book by a favorite male author and reading: "Every woman, whether rich or poor, married or single, has a circle of influence, within which, according to her character, she is exerting a certain amount of power for good or harm. Every woman, by her virtue or her vice; by her folly or her wisdom; by her levity or her dignity, is adding something to our national elevation or degradation."[8]

Imagine your daughter perusing a catalog from Mt. Holyoke Female Seminary and being "promised an education that would render women handmaidens to the gospel and provide them with tools they could use 'in the great task of renovating the world.'"[9]

Imagine getting a copy of the much-talked-about *Democracy in America* and reading: ". . . if I were asked, now that I am drawing to the close of this work, in which I have spoken of so many important things done by the Americans, to what the singular prosperity and growing strength of that people ought mainly to be attributed, I should reply: To the superiority of their women."[10]

It sounds idyllic.

But that is not the time in history when God placed *us* on this planet. That was then; this is now.

Fast forward from the nineteenth century to the end of the twentieth century and imagine . . .

My friend Ruth returning to teach high school after thirteen years as a stay-at-home mom. "I knew intellectually about the notion of truth being relative, but I was not prepared for the reality of the results of this philosophy. In a discussion about cheating, I told the students they should not cheat because it was wrong. They could not connect with what I was saying. They looked at me incredulously and asked, 'Why?'"

Faithful Christian parents being told by their teenage daughter that she is pregnant and wants to have an abortion. It is an easy way to "get rid of the problem," and she thinks their objections are just another ploy to control her.

My young friend Jennifer, along with seventeen other students in a high school health class in a conservative suburban community, being asked if they think it is wrong for an unmarried couple to live together. Jennifer and five others said yes. Two-thirds saw no problem with this arrangement.

A Re-imagining Conference billed as "A Global Conference by Women; for Women and Men," where conference participants reportedly explored ways to "re-imagine" God in nontraditional ways. One speaker told the group, "I don't think we need a theory of atonement at all. I think Jesus came for life and to show us something about life. . . . I don't think we need folks hanging on crosses and blood dripping and weird stuff . . . " Participants worshiped the divine in each other by marking red dots on their foreheads to signify their divinity and then bowing to each other in an act of reverence. They sang songs to the goddess Sophia, the source of their divinity, the creator who dwells within them and unleashes within them their divine power.[11]

A United Nations World Conference on Women in Beijing, China, where, according to Dr. James Dobson: ". . . the delegates from the United States, Canada and the European Union lived up to expectations. They focused on redesigning the family, reordering the way males and females interrelate, promoting 'reproductive rights for women,' distributing condoms and safe-sex nonsense to kids, propagating 'homosexual and lesbian rights,' weakening parental authority, undermining 'patriarchal' religious teachings and spreading feminist ideology to every nation on earth."[12] Workshops at the conference included "Lesbian Flirtation Techniques Workshop" and "How Religious Fundamentalism Helps the Spread of AIDS."

Obviously the reasons for such a contrast between then and now are complex. But the question must be asked: Is the loss of true womanhood a basic cause for our current cultural poverty and confusion? It seems undeniable that it is at least a contributor. Which forces another question: Could the recapturing of true womanhood be a contributor to, or dare we dream, a catalyst for reforming and reshaping culture?

The true-woman concept is much broader than the husband-and-wife relationship. We will see that the virtues of true womanhood are biblical virtues that cross all cultural, situational, and generational boundaries and go to the heart of the covenant community of faith. But first let me build a case for the urgency for women of biblical faith to give a true reflection of our redemption by maintaining a firm and uncorrupted virtue that "will stand sentinel over that of the empire" at this time in history.

OUR TIME

Cultural chaos is nothing new. Since Adam and Eve plunged humanity into sin, there have been two kingdoms warring over territorial rights. The territory is man's heart, and the issue is who will rule. There is no demilitarized zone. The enemy of our souls is ruthless, deceptive, and dazzling. He cunningly adapts to each generation and location. But in God's providence, this is the time in history and the place on the globe that He has placed us. This is the time and place that we are to reflect our redemption. So what characterizes our time?

Peggy Noonan, former speechwriter for Ronald Reagan and George Bush, gave a trenchant critique in *Forbes* magazine. Her critique is noteworthy because of her vantage point that affords her the opportunity to observe and participate in the broader secular culture. In a sense, this is a view from within. Noonan writes: "The life of people on earth is obviously much better than it was 500 years ago. . . . But we are not happier. I believe we are just cleaner, more attractive sad people than we used to be."[13]

After cataloging some reasons people today are discontented, Noonan declares:

> It is embarrassing to live in the most comfortable time in the history of man and not be happy. We all have so much!
> ... I find myself thinking of Auden's words about the average man in 1939, as darkness gathered over Europe. ... Auden called his era the "age of anxiety." I think what was at the heart of the dread in those days, just a few years into modern times, was that we could tell we were beginning to lose God—banishing him from the scene, from our consciousness, losing the assumption that he was part of the daily drama, or its maker. And it is a terrible thing when people lose God. Life is difficult and people are afraid, and to be without God is to lose man's great source of consolation and coherence. ...
> I don't think it is unconnected to the boomers' predicament that as a country we were losing God just as they were being born.
> At the same time, a huge revolution in human expectation was beginning to shape our lives, the salient feature of which is the expectation of happiness. ...
> Somewhere in the seventies, or the sixties, we started expecting to be happy, and changed our lives (left town, left families, switched jobs) if we were not. And society strained and cracked in the storm.
> I think we have lost the old knowledge that happiness is overrated—that, in a way, life is overrated. We have lost, somehow, a sense of mystery—about us, our purpose, our meaning, our role. Our ancestors believed in two worlds, and understood this to be the solitary, poor, nasty, brutish and short one. We are the first generations of man that actually expected to find happiness here on earth, and our search for it has caused such—unhappiness. The reason: If you do not believe in another, higher world, if you believe only in the flat material world around you, if you believe that this is your

only chance at happiness—if that is what you believe, then you are not disappointed when the world does not give you a good measure of its riches—you are despairing.[14]

After this piercing analysis of our time, Noonan concludes on a note of what sounds to me to be sad resignation:

> It's odd to accuse boomers of reticence, but I think we have been reticent, at least in this:
>
> When we talk about the difficulties of our lives and how our country has changed, we become embarrassed and feel . . . dotty. Like someone's old aunt rocking on the porch and talking about the good old days. And so most of us keep quiet, raise our children as best we can, go to the cocktail party, eat our cake, go to work and take the vacation.
>
> We have removed ourselves from leadership, we professional white-collar boomers. We have recused ourselves from a world we never made. We turn our attention to the arts and entertainment, to watching and supporting them or contributing to them, because they are the only places we can imagine progress. And to money, hoping that it will keep us safe.[15]

The oddity of our time is the juxtaposition of Peggy Noonan's commentary and the rise of evangelicalism. On the one hand there is this discontent and reticent resignation, and on the other hand we hear staggering statistics about the growth of evangelicalism. David Wells comments on this:

> The vast growth in evangelically minded people in the 1960s, 1970s, and 1980s should by now have revolutionized American culture. With a third of American adults now claiming to have experienced spiritual rebirth, a powerful countercurrent of morality growing out of a powerful and alternative worldview should have been unleashed in factories, offices,

and boardrooms, in the media, universities, and professions, from one end of the country to the other. The results should by now be unmistakable. Secular values should be reeling, and those who are their proponents should be very troubled. But as it turns out, all of this swelling of the evangelical ranks has passed unnoticed in the culture. It has simply been absorbed and tamed. . . . This surely is an odd circumstance. Here is a corner of the religious world that has learned from the social scientists how to grow itself, that is sprouting huge megachurches that look like shopping malls for the religious, that can count in its own society the moneyed and powerful, and yet it causes not so much as a ripple. . . . Thus it is that both American culture and American evangelicalism have come to share the same fate, both basking in the same stunning, outward success while stricken by a painful vacuity, an emptiness in their respective centers. . . . In the one there are no moral absolutes, and in the other there is no theology.[16]

OUR OPPORTUNITY

This is our time. This is our opportunity. There is a vacuum of moral leadership. There is decadence and despair. There is a shallowness of theology that has produced a superficial lifestyle among Christians. But woman is the keeper of the moral atmosphere. She sets the moral compass. But not just any woman.

The author of *Female Piety* understood this:

> Man is neither safe in himself, nor profitable to others, when he lives dissociated from that benign influence which is to be found in woman's presence and character. . . . But it is not woman, gay, frivolous, and unbelieving, or woman separated from those divine teachings which make all hearts wise, that can lay claim to the exercise of such an influence. But when she adds to the traits of sympathy, forbearance, and warm affection, which characterize her, the strength and wisdom of a

well-cultivated intellect, and the still higher attributes of religious faith and holy love, it is not easy to limit the good she may do in all situations, and in all periods of life.[17]

A Band-Aid approach will not suffice. Our moment in history demands women who know their time, but who are not controlled or manipulated by their time. Our time begs for women of biblical faith who can exert a reforming influence on culture.

In my work as consultant for the women's ministry of my denomination, I spend much energy exploring the role of women in the home, church, and world and training women to fulfill their calling. At a leadership training conference, a woman asked an insightful and heartfelt question: "As we pursue our desire to train women for kingdom work through the women's ministry of our churches, what is to keep us from spinning out of control and going the way of so many other women's movements? Is it wise for us to organize and mobilize women?"

I had considered these questions and was prepared to answer, or so I thought. My response: "Women *will* organize, and they *will* mobilize. If we *don't* give biblical leadership, there will be a vacuum, and someone will fill it. A laissez-faire approach may suffice for a season, but eventually someone will become frustrated and erupt, and others will follow. Anger-birthed leadership is dangerous."

Following the meeting, the question hovered over me. I could not disentangle it from my brain. I finally concluded that there was another part of the answer that God wanted me to learn.

It took a lot of soul-excavation before I went deep enough to unearth the treasure I found. It was hard work. At times my spiritual muscles ached. I was weary from this soul-work, and I was uncertain that I had made the right discovery, so I went to visit Rosalie. That visit was the final push to write this book.

Rosalie Cassels is a fascinating woman. She is one of my heroines and one of my spiritual mothers. In her late eighties, she is full of wisdom and grace that has come from living a life of serving her Savior through His church.

Rosalie was born January 1, 1907. She has been a member of Rose Hill Presbyterian Church in Columbia, South Carolina, since she was about eight years old. Her father began this church as a Sunday school class for poor children.

As Rosalie became a young woman, she had a passion for training women to serve the Lord through His church. She held many positions in the women's work of her denomination. Her husband was a prominent and successful businessman, so she had the resources to travel to mission fields encouraging missionaries.

But of all the things Rosalie did, her eyes light up the most when she tells about serving as Director of the Interdenominational Christian Conference for Negro Women at Benedict College. This was a week-long summer program to train black women for kingdom work. Rosalie's tenure in this volunteer position spanned the years from 1947-1967. Think about it—this was before racial reconciliation was in vogue. A couple of years after she began this work, her maid became ill while the family was vacationing at their lake house. Rosalie drove her into town to see the doctor. On the way, the maid needed to use the restroom. Rosalie made several stops, but there was no place that would allow a black woman to use their facilities. By the time they reached Columbia, Rosalie had a new mission. Though her cause was unpopular in her community at that time, she worked tirelessly to improve the circumstances of blacks.

I have sat spellbound as Rosalie told me incredible stories, usually not even aware that the stories were extraordinary. This particular afternoon she told me that during the time she worked in interracial ministries, she would often go into churches or restaurants, and she could see and hear people whispering. "I could feel their disapproval," she said. "But it didn't matter. I was doing what God told me to do."

Then I asked about the Bible class she taught in her church for forty years. She was more interested in telling me about Bennie, one of her housekeepers who is teaching a Sunday school class in her church. And then, with delight dancing in her eyes, Rosalie told me that every Saturday she and Bennie sit on the couch with Rosalie's books spread around them. Rosalie is teaching Bennie how to use Bible study helps and how to plan a lesson.

This true woman is like the Energizer Bunny—she keeps going and going. She seizes whatever opportunity God gives her. Rosalie's physical heart may be weaker, but her heart for the Lord and for His church is stronger because her character is shaped and driven by God's Spirit and His Word.

Sitting in her presence, I knew I had made the right discovery regarding the potential danger of equipping and mobilizing women for kingdom service.

Any group is in danger of spinning out of control unless each individual woman's redeemed character is shaped and driven by God's Spirit and His Word.

Placing a high premium on each woman's character is mandatory for a group of women to stay on course. Godly leadership keeps this foundational principle at the center. It is godly character that will persevere and finish well regardless of the opposition or obstacles.

My discovery seems obvious. It is not a complicated truth, but it is a core truth. Perhaps its simplicity causes us to take it for granted. We assume everyone knows it. And then it slips to the background, and soon everyone has forgotten it.

We must train women to serve the King of the church through His church because of who He is—the King of glory; and we must continually remind them who they are—His redeemed daughters.

A CLOSE ENCOUNTER

We will explore the standard, the identity, and the virtues of the true woman in later chapters. But let me set the stage by presenting a breathtaking scene from Scripture that I want to hold before you as we begin our quest into what it means to be a true woman.

The Lord God spoke to our spiritual father Abraham and made an extraordinary promise: "I will establish my covenant as an everlasting covenant between me and you and your descendants after you for the generations to come, to be your God and the God of your descendants after you" (Genesis 17:7).

"Your descendants" includes me! All believers are spiritual descendants of Abraham, so the God of glory is *my* God.

And it keeps getting better. "I will put my dwelling place among you, and I will not abhor you. I will walk among you and be your God, and you will be my people" (Leviticus 26:11-12).

He will not be an absentee father. He will live among us. We will be His people and live in His presence.

Keep this promise in mind as we look at the scene at Mt. Sinai. Try to form a mental picture of this amazing episode. The thunder and lightning, the thick cloud over the mountain, the loud trumpet blast, smoke billowing up as though from a furnace, the mountain trembling violently, the trumpet getting louder and louder—this goes beyond awesome (Exodus 19:16-19). But while Moses is on the mountain receiving God's law, the people make and worship a golden calf. In response to this flagrant disobedience, God strikes the people with a plague and says to Moses, ". . . Go up to the land flowing with milk and honey. But I will not go with you, because you are a stiff-necked people and I might destroy you on the way" (Exodus 33:3).

The plague was one thing, but when God said, "I will not go with you," Moses panicked. God was threatening to withdraw His presence, and that was the one thing Moses knew they could not do without. Moses could not deny that the people were rebellious; he could only plead God's covenant faithfulness to be their God and to live among them. So he cried, "Remember that this nation is your people" (Exodus 33:13).

"The Lord replied, 'My Presence will go with you, and I will give you rest.'

"Then Moses said to him, 'If your Presence does not go with us, do not send us up from here. How will anyone know that you are pleased with me and with your people unless you go with us?

What else will distinguish me and your people from all the other people on the face of the earth?'" (Exodus 33:14-16).

Then Moses made the ultimate request: "Show me your glory." And God did.

Moses spent forty days on the mountain with the Lord. Following this incredible encounter, when he returned to the people with the tablets of the Law in his hands, "he was not aware that his face was radiant because he had spoken with the Lord" (Exodus 34:29).

Moses' world was as cluttered with unbelief, rebellion, and moral collapse as our world today. But he knew that all that mattered was: "If your Presence does not go with us, do not send us up from here."

Moses knew that the only thing that would distinguish them from everyone else on the face of the earth was God dwelling among them.

And when Moses spent time in the glorious presence of God, he radiated that glory. Such a close encounter with glory could not be repressed; it could only be reflected.

IN SUMMARY

When my friend Sharon Kraemer was diagnosed with cancer, her response was, "I am confident that God will use this to take me deeper into His love for me." I didn't see Sharon until several weeks after surgery and several rounds of chemotherapy, and at my first sight of her I gasped. It was not because her body and her hair were so thin. My shock was because Sharon absolutely glowed with peace and love. She was awash with an undeniable radiance. I could only exclaim, "Sharon, you must have been spending some incredible times with the Lord." She did not need to reply. The evidence was there.

This is the essence of the true woman. Regardless of the time in history when she inhabits this earth, she is one who lives in the presence of glory. Her redeemed character is shaped and driven by God's Word and Spirit. Because she is the very dwelling place of the

Lord God, her reflection of Him is manifested in every relationship and circumstance of life. The distinguishing characteristic of her life is His presence in her radiating out to all who see her. The true woman's life is not segmented into sacred and secular. All of life is sacred because it is lived in His presence. The true woman is a true reflection of God's glory.

Personal Reflection

1. I must begin by asking you to "examine yourself to see whether you are in the faith" (2 Corinthians 13:5). Are you trusting in Christ alone for your salvation? Have you repented of your sin and put your faith in His life of perfect obedience and His atoning sacrifice on the cross? He is the source of truth, for He is truth, and it is only as you are in relationship with Him that you can reflect Him. Write a statement of your faith in your journal.

2. Are you a participating member of a worshiping community? Have you placed yourself under the authority of a local church?

3. Read Acts 17:26-28 and reflect on the truth that God sovereignly determined the time in history when, and the place on the planet where, you would live. Meditate on the fact that in Him you "live and move and have your being." Record your thoughts in your journal.

4. Read and meditate on Exodus 33 and 34. Ask God to show you His glory. Record your thoughts.

5. Read 1 Corinthians 3:16 and praise God that He is not an absentee father. His dwelling place is among you—indeed He dwells in you. Again record your thoughts about this glorious truth.

REFLECTING REDEMPTION
AS A

W I D O W

"I'm sorry, we did all we could; he didn't make it." This was not the message I had prayed for or expected. My precious husband was suddenly dead at age forty-four.

As the harsh reality of the doctor's words penetrated my numbed mind and heart, God's Spirit brought His Word to me. Our faithful God gave me the gift of faith, and I heard my own voice saying, "Blessed be the name of the Lord." Words cannot describe the overwhelming sense of loss or the overwhelming peace that flooded over me. It amazes me how God, in His sovereignty, providentially prepared my heart for that very moment and the next hours, days, nights, months, and years.

As a teen, I lived with my paternal grandmother the summer following my grandfather's death. God used that time to prepare me for this life and for eternity. My grandmother helped me understand my need for a Savior. She also taught me much about faith as I heard her call on God for grace and praise Him for His faithfulness as she walked through deep grief.

As a young couple, my husband and I heard a widow of one week testify to God's faithfulness. It was a compelling witness to hear her read the hymn "Be Still, My Soul."

> *Be still, my soul: the Lord is on thy side;*
> *Bear patiently the cross of grief or pain;*
> *Leave to thy God to order and provide;*

In every change He faithful will remain.
Be still, my soul: thy best, thy heavenly Friend
Thro' thorny ways leads to a joyful end.

The words of that hymn ministered to us mightily then and many times through the years that followed.

A number of years later my weekly Bible study included one other married woman; all the others were widows. Week after week I heard their testimonies of God's provision and grace as they struggled with the many adjustments of widowhood. I remembered those women the day my husband died and reminded myself that God had brought them through and that He could do the same for me.

I am thankful that personal Bible study, time spent with my husband in the Word, and being part of a church where the Word was faithfully taught had been a very important part of my life. This solid foundation gave me focus, strength, and great peace.

The morning my husband was dying, my women's Bible study was meeting, and they immediately went to prayer. I am convinced that their prayer support helped me keep my eyes on the Lord rather than on the circumstances. Of course, there were times when I had to beg God to give me the faith and grace to trust. I did not understand or like His plan, but I knew He loved me with a redemptive love. I knew He was and is completely sovereign, infinite in wisdom, and perfect in love.

As a testimony to my husband's faith, I requested two congregational hymns at his memorial service, "Hallelujah, What a Savior" and, of course, "Be Still, My Soul."

Be still, my soul: when dearest friends depart,
And all is darkened in the vale of tears,
Then shalt thou better know His love, His heart,
Who comes to soothe thy sorrow and thy fears.
Be still, my soul: thy Jesus can repay
From His own fullness all He takes away.

God's Spirit enabled me to obediently trust Him. My obedience included saturating myself in the Word when I didn't "feel" like it. As time passed, sometimes the grief was so overwhelming I found it difficult to concentrate. During one of those times, God gave me the wonderful gift of the following verses. "Find rest, O my soul, in God alone; my hope comes from him. He alone is my rock and my salvation; he is my fortress, I will not be shaken. My salvation and my honor depend on God; he is my mighty rock, my refuge. Trust in him at all times, O people; pour out your hearts to him, for God is our refuge" (Psalm 62:5-8).

In an instant, God changed the course of my life and ministry. Did God change? No. Did God's plan for me change? No. Did God keep His promise to be with me and never to forsake me? Yes. Did God provide for our three children and me? Yes. Have there been difficult times? Yes. Has God's grace been sufficient? Yes.

God has remained faithful, and by His grace, it has been exciting to continue on the journey He planned for me before the foundation of the world. He has given us so many promises, but two are very special to me as a widow: "For your Maker is your husband—the Lord Almighty is his name—the Holy One of Israel is your Redeemer" (Isaiah 54:5). "'Though the mountains be shaken and the hills be removed, yet my unfailing love for you will not be shaken nor my covenant of peace be removed,' says the Lord, who has compassion on you" (Isaiah 54:10).

So I still sing,

> Be still, my soul: the hour is hast'ning on
>   When we shall be forever with the Lord,
> When disappointment, grief, and fear are gone,
>   Sorrow forgot, love's purest joys restored.
> Be still, my soul: when change and tears are past,
>   All safe and blessed we shall meet at last. Amen.

—*Ann Llewelyn,*
Atlanta, GA

ℋER STANDARD

Christianity has provided a place for woman for which she is fitted, and in which she shines; but take her out of that place, and her lustre pales and sheds a feeble and sickly ray.

Female Piety

The true woman's purpose is God's glory. Her standard to determine how to fulfill her purpose is God's Word. The first two questions of The Westminster Shorter Catechism state clearly and concisely that fulfilling our purpose is inextricably bound to God's Word.

Question: What is the chief end of man?
Answer: Man's chief end is to glorify God and to enjoy Him forever.
Question: What rule hath God given to direct us how we may glorify and enjoy Him?
Answer: The word of God, which is contained in the Scriptures of the Old and New Testaments, is the only rule to direct us how we may glorify and enjoy Him.[1]

The true woman's infallible rule for faith and practice is God's Word.

The new woman's rule for faith and practice is her experience.

This produces a hedonistic pursuit of pleasure that makes her an obscene caricature of true womanhood.

How did this switch from the true to the new happen?

A PRODUCT OF THEOLOGY

Barbara Welter contends that the true-woman concept "carried within itself the seeds of its own destruction. For if woman was so very little less than the angels, she should surely take a more active part in running the world, especially since men were making such a hash of things. Real women often felt they did not live up to the ideal of True Womanhood: some of them blamed themselves, some challenged the standard, some tried to keep the virtues and enlarge the scope of womanhood. Somehow through this mixture of challenge and acceptance, of change and continuity, the True Woman evolved into the New Woman—a transformation as startling in its way as the abolition of slavery or the coming of the machine age. And yet the stereotype, the 'mystique' if you will, of what woman was and ought to be persisted, bringing guilt and confusion in the midst of opportunity."[2]

So Welter's explanation for the dissolution of the true-woman concept was that the concept itself was flawed. I beg to disagree.

I contend that the true woman and the new woman are both products of their theology. They both have a worldview determined by their theology. Theology is simply the study of God. The true became the new when the biblical truth about God was compromised.

Before we consider how the true became the new, let's think about how the concept of true womanhood developed in the first place.

The defining virtues of true womanhood (piety, purity, domesticity, and submission) are biblical virtues. Many of the early settlers of America, including the women, were rooted in Puritan theology. My contention is that it was the seeds of this theology that produced the true-woman concept.

In *A Quest for Godliness: The Puritan Vision of the Christian Life*,
J. I. Packer answers the question that you may be asking: What's the
big deal about the Puritans? What did they have that we need?
Packer's answer:

> The answer, in one word, is maturity. Maturity is a com-
> pound of wisdom, goodwill, resilience, and creativity. The
> Puritans exemplified maturity; we don't. We are spiritual
> dwarfs. . . . They were great souls serving a great God. In them
> clear-headed passion and warm-hearted compassion com-
> bined. Visionary and practical, idealistic and realistic too,
> goal-oriented and methodical, they were great believers, great
> hopers, great doers, and great sufferers. But their sufferings
> . . . seasoned and ripened them till they gained a stature that
> was nothing short of heroic. Ease and luxury, such as our
> affluence brings us today, do not make for maturity; hardship
> and struggle however do, and the Puritans' battles against the
> spiritual and climatic wildernesses in which God set them
> produced a virility of character, undaunted and unsinkable,
> rising above discouragement and fears. . . .
> The Puritans lost, more or less, every public battle that they
> fought. Those who stayed in England did not change the
> Church of England as they hoped to do, nor did they revive
> more than a minority of its adherents, and eventually they
> were driven out of Anglicanism by calculated pressure on
> their consciences. Those who crossed the Atlantic failed to
> establish new Jerusalem in New England; for the first fifty
> years their little colonies barely survived. They hung on by
> the skin of their teeth. But the moral and spiritual victories
> that the Puritans won by keeping sweet, peaceful, patient,
> obedient, and hopeful under sustained and seemingly intol-
> erable pressures and frustrations give them a place of high
> honour in the believers' hall of fame, where Hebrews 11 is the
> first gallery.[3]

Puritan theology dominated the assembly called by Parliament in 1643 to settle matters regarding the government and liturgy of the Church of England. This assembly met at Westminster Abbey in London. Thus the document they crafted is known as The Westminster Confession of Faith. It has been said that:

> . . . the Long Parliament had the opportunity to select a body for the work of creed construction, fitter therefore than could have been found in any other age in England down to this day, perhaps. Puritanism had been doing its work of making great men in England for a century. . . . The middle of the seventeenth century was, from a moral and spiritual point of view, the greatest age in the history of England to the present. Under the providence of God, the Long Parliament had the noblest age of England to choose the Assembly from; and it chose well as has appeared.[4]

That assembly began its work by asserting the authority of Scripture. That is the starting point. If we are deficient in our view of Scripture, we will be inferior on every other point. The first chapter of The Westminster Confession of Faith states: "The authority of the Holy Scripture, for which it ought to be believed, and obeyed, dependeth not upon the testimony of any man, or Church; but wholly upon God (who is truth itself) the author thereof; and therefore it is to be received, because it is the Word of God."[5]

The third question of The Westminster Shorter Catechism asks:

Question: What do the Scriptures principally teach?
Answer: The Scriptures principally teach what man is to believe concerning God, and what duty God requires of man.[6]

Early American Christians were fortified with this strong, systematic approach to faith and life. They looked to Scripture to find out what they should believe and how they should behave. They viewed their world and their life through the lens of Scripture, so biblical truth was integrated into all of life. And this, I believe, is the foundation of the true-woman concept.

Let's consider the lives of two women who exemplified this concept. Both were products of Puritan theology.

EXAMPLES OF TRUE WOMEN

Mary Fish is a bridge between our founding mothers and the true woman of the first half of the nineteenth century. She lived from 1736 to 1818. Her story is told in the book *The Way of Duty: A Woman and Her Family in Revolutionary America.*

There are few firsthand accounts of seventeenth- and eighteenth-century women. Survival took precedence over recording their thoughts and experiences. But Mary kept a journal and a book of "Reminiscences." Her youngest son, Benjamin Silliman, the most influential scientist in America during the early nineteenth century and the first professor of chemistry at Yale, preserved his mother's writings and collected as much of her correspondence as he could. "He prefaced the document with a recommendation that all her descendants cherish her words and follow her example, and he took pains to circulate it among all branches of the family."[7]

Her father was a New England preacher. Her parents had a deep influence on her life. Mary wrote:

> They were very watchful over us in all our ways, and they had such a happy mode of governing that they would even govern us with an eye, and they never used severity with us at all. . . . My father's practice was every day to take us into his study, immediately after family prayers in the morning, and hear us read, and he would give us advice for the day. He would also enjoin it upon us to read our Bibles by ourselves every day. . . . The Sabbath we were taught to keep with the greatest strictness, both at home and in the house of God and on our way to and from the same, not allowing us to walk or

ride with those who would talk of worldly matters on the Lord's day. . . . They taught us also to call ourselves to account every night . . . to forgive injuries, and if any one spoke evil of us, we must examine ourselves and see wherein we had been culpable, and if we found we had done wrong, to be sorry for it, and resolve never to do so any more, but if we found [ourselves] innocent . . . never to return railing for railing [but] pray God to forgive our enemies . . . always to be glad if we could oblige even the most unobliging and to be thankful when it lay in our power to do any kind of office for any of our fellow creatures. They early taught us diligence—that we must always be doing something that would turn out to profit . . . and I feared that my father should at any time find me doing nothing, lest he should put the question, What? are you idle my child?[8]

A high sense of duty was characteristic of the Puritans, and the duty motif was dominant for Mary Fish. It is seen in a letter from her second husband shortly after their engagement: "Happy, Happy Hour will that be, my Dearest of all created Blessings, that shall unite our happy Souls & Bodies in the blessed Bonds of Marriage and enable us to walk through all the Scenes of this Life mutually supporting, blessing & assisting Each other in the Way of Duty, until we shall at last be called off the Stage to enjoy an Eternity of Happiness in the World of blessed Spirits above."[9]

But it was her father who taught her that "the way of duty is the way of safety."

In 1776 Mary wrote to her parents: "I tell you with a heart most tenderly affected that this morning an express comes in with orders from the Governor for my dearest Beloved to march forthwith to New York with a part of his regiment, there to wait for the arrival of General Washington. What I have long feared is now come upon me; I endeavour to commit him to the care of a kind providence, hoping he may be returned in safety."[10]

Her father replied: "Where should our Friends be, and where

are they safest, but there, where the Lord calls them, where their Duty lies? There only may we hope for & expect protection, even where we are serving God, according to his Will. I therefore look on Mr. Silliman safer now, in the Army, where called, than at home, in his Chair, while his Call abroad continues."[11]

The duty theme appears again in 1805 in a letter to her son Benjamin when he left to study in England: "After following you with my eyes as far as I could see your sulky, I retired into the house with the consoling thought that you was going, where providence calls you, and the way of duty is the way of safety."[12]

Two years before her death, she wrote of her great concern for family worship: "They [the children] should be taught when family worship is performed to lay all by and sit in a decent posture to read or hear God's word read, and not be looking out of the window or playing with any thing about them, and instead of bustle and motion about the house, it ought to be like that of Cornelius, who said to Peter 'here are we all before thee to hear what thou shalt say unto us.'"[13]

Her son Benjamin wrote of her: "She was a heroic woman and encountered with firmness the trials and terrors of the American Revolution in which my father was largely concerned. . . . In her widowhood, after my father's death in 1790, she struggled on in embarrassed circumstances & gave my brother & myself a public education, forming our minds at home to purity & piety. Whatever I have of good in me I owe under God mainly to her."[14]

The book is fascinating, but I was particularly intrigued by the authors' conclusion: "She died on the second of July, 1818, and appropriately for a woman of her generation, she was committed to the American earth on the anniversary of her country's independence. Yet she remained to the end of her life *less a daughter of the Revolution than a child of the Puritans.*"[15] (italics mine)

Elizabeth Prentiss was born the year Mary Fish died. She, too, was a child of the Puritans. In *The Life and Letters of Elizabeth Prentiss,* her husband wrote that her father "belonged to a very old Puritan

stock."[16] It has been written of her that she "grew up within sanctified air."[17]

She, too, emphasized the duty/safety motif. In a letter to a
friend she wrote:

> Holiness is not a mere abstraction; it is praying and loving
> and being consecrated, but it is also the doing kind deeds,
> speaking friendly words, being in a crowd when we thirst to
> be alone, and so on and so on. . . . For we can do nothing well
> unless we do it consciously for Christ, and this consciousness
> sometimes gets jostled out of us when we undertake to do too
> much. The more perfectly He is formed in us the more light we
> shall get on every path of duty, the less likely to go astray from
> the happy medium of not all contemplation, not all activity.[18]

In a letter to another friend she wrote: "I have felt about hymns
just as you say you do, as if I loved them more than the Bible. But
I have got over that; I prayed myself out of it, not loving hymns the
less, but the Bible more."[19]

Five years before her death, she wrote to a young relative: "To
love Christ more—this is the deepest need, the constant cry of my
soul. Down in the bowling-alley, and out in the woods, and on my
bed, and out driving, when I am happy and busy, and when I am
sad and idle, the whisper keeps going up for more love, more love,
more love."[20]

This driving passion of her life is expressed in her hymn "More
Love to Thee" and chronicled in her book *Stepping Heavenward*.

My conclusion is that the nineteenth-century true woman was
a child of the Puritans. Her theology produced a way of life that
evoked admiration and respect. Tocqueville was so struck with this
that he wrote:

> In the United States men seldom compliment women, but
> they daily show how much they esteem them. They con-
> stantly display an entire confidence in the understanding of a

wife and a profound respect for her freedom; they have decided that her mind is just as fitted as that of a man to discover the plain truth, and her heart as firm to embrace it; and they have never sought to place her virtue, any more than his, under the shelter of prejudice, ignorance, and fear. . . . their conduct to women always implies that they suppose them to be virtuous and refined; and such is the respect entertained for the moral freedom of the sex that in the presence of a woman the most guarded language is used lest her ear should be offended by an expression.[21]

THE TRUE DISPLACED BY THE NEW

How did the true woman give way to the new woman?

I maintain that when the theology was tweaked, the concept collapsed. In the second half of the nineteenth century, the dominant theology became experience-based rather than truth-based. David Wells gives this analysis of the theological shift that occurred:

> . . . beginning in 1792, the breath of revival was experienced in the towns and villages along the Connecticut River valley. The initial gust eventually grew into a storm in the 1820s and 1830s, and though it tapered off later, it continued to blow in different places and times all the way down to the end of the century. This Second Great Awakening ushered in the new Age of Protestantism. The age was new not only in the extent to which Protestant belief affected the nation but in its theological temper as well. The Puritan establishment had been formed around Calvinistic beliefs, and it was these, sans their political outworkings, that were given new life under Jonathan Edwards in the First Great Awakening of the eighteenth century. The second half of the nineteenth century, by contrast, saw the emergence of a pervasive Arminianism, which as George Marsden has noted, was a way of thinking

that was thoroughly in step with the active, confident, and democratic mood in the country. Achieving a perfect embodiment in Charles Finney, this revivalistic Arminianism eventually stifled, if not supplanted, the older form of Reformation thinking, and it has continued to flow through our own century, losing depth as it has gained breadth, finally spilling out over most of contemporary evangelicalism.[22]

As objective biblical truth was replaced by subjective internal experience, the emphasis shifted from God to man. And the true woman became an illusion. The virtues that were rooted in sound theology could not stand the strain of self-absorption. Without a theological anchor, the true woman concept became a form of godliness (outward behavior) without the substance of godliness (inner convictions). Her character ceased to be shaped and driven by God's Word. She became artificial.

Form without substance is froth, and it evaporates as easily and quickly as the foam in a bubble bath. So by the twentieth century, woman was ripe for all of the new philosophies coming down the pike.

New ideas take time to work themselves from the philosophers to the populace to the pew. But secularism slithered its way into the hearts of women through the messages of feminism. Elizabeth Prentiss breathed sanctified air, but twentieth-century women have breathed feminist air for so long that we have absorbed an egocentric, relativistic worldview into our souls without even realizing it. Modernity has taken its toll on womanhood, and the new woman has displaced the true woman. It is not a pretty picture.

This defection is not just among non-Christian women. Consider these conversations I have had with women who Sunday after Sunday sit on the pews of evangelical churches.

"My husband left me. My unmarried daughter is pregnant. I have always tried to serve God, and what has it gotten me? I don't deserve this."

"I have never been happy in this marriage. It just isn't working. I know God doesn't want me to be unhappy. I guess it was never meant to be."

"My church doesn't meet my needs. No one reaches out to me, and I don't like the pastor. He preaches from the Bible, but his sermons are boring. I see no reason to keep going."

"My husband doesn't understand me. He is absorbed with his career. I know divorce is wrong, but there's got to be more to life than this. I want to have some fun! I am going to start thinking about myself and do things for me. I'll just let him live his life, and I'll live mine."

"We had looked forward to our retirement. We planned to travel and even go on some mission trips. Now my husband's mother has had a stroke, and we have to care for her. It just doesn't seem fair."

"Jeff is pressuring me to move in with him. I know it's probably not right, but I'm thirty-five years old and single. I want a husband and baby. I'm afraid if I don't agree, he'll leave. We do love each other, and he says he is a Christian. It can't be that wrong, and surely once I am pregnant he will want to get married."

"My husband has been unemployed for six months. He has been able to do some part-time work to pay the bills, but I feel overwhelmed with the financial pressure. I resent my friends who have no financial problems, and I can't understand why God doesn't do something."

"My childhood was so painful. There is no way I can forgive those who hurt me. I am often depressed, and no one seems to understand how hard it is for me."

This is the voice of the new woman in the body of the Christian woman. This is unrestrained, immature selfism. I don't mean to stand in judgment of others. What is so terrifying is that too often this is my voice.

Mary Fish and Elizabeth Prentiss endured the pain of widowhood, war, death of children, financial collapse, depression, and poor health. But the entries in their journals show that their approach to these trials stands in stark contrast to the litany of woes listed above from my conversations with women.

Let me hasten to say that there are scores of women today who do have deep theological roots and whose lives clearly reflect the fruit. There are women who view their lives through the lens of Scripture rather than through the lens of their experience. I deliberately chose contemporary stories to open each chapter of this book because I am so moved by the true women of our day. But it does seem that the pervasive mood is one of selfism and that we must grapple with the virtues of the true woman, seek to understand them in light of Scripture, and live them in every nook and cranny of our lives.

VERITABLE OR VIRTUAL REALITY

Being a true woman in today's culture means moving from casual observation to trench warfare. An experience-based approach will not empower women for this kind of conflict. Being a true woman demands fearless fealty to the authority of Scripture.

Fidelity to God's Word was the issue Mother Eve faced in the very first temptation. When Satan shrewdly asked, "Hath God said . . . " (Genesis 3:1), he was casting doubt over the veracity and authority of God's Word. When Eve yielded, veritable reality became virtual reality; the true became the almost true. And almost true is untrue. Sin brought distortion, destruction, and death. The issue has been the same in every age: Hath God said?

The unquestionable authority of God's Word must be our standard. When we deviate from God's truth, we lose touch with what is real. The slightest deviation from God's truth produces a counterfeit reality that makes us vulnerable to the lure of culture.

David Wells describes the effects of this departure from biblical truth on today's church:

> The disappearance of theology from the life of the church
> . . . is hard to miss today . . . in the vacuous worship that is so
> prevalent, for example, in the shift from God to the self as the
> central focus of faith, in the psychologized preaching that fol-

lows this shift, in the erosion of its conviction, in its strident pragmatism, in its inability to think incisively about the culture, in its reveling in the irrational. And it would have made few of these capitulations to modernity had not its capacity for truth diminished.[23]

But the veritable reality is that "All Scripture is God-breathed and is useful for teaching, rebuking, correcting and training in righteousness, so that the man [and woman] of God may be thoroughly equipped for every good work" (2 Timothy 3:16).

We will only be an authentic Masterpiece when we line up with God's truth.

WOMEN OF VALOR

I am not suggesting a return to a Puritan or Victorian age. The "good old days" when womanhood was valued may sound serene and secure, but these women faced enormous obstacles. The difference between then and now is that Mary Fish and Elizabeth Prentiss were the norm. They flowed with the culture. Their challenges were different from ours, but according to Tocqueville, these women faced their hurdles with valor. After noting that the American ethic and commerce required married women to sacrifice their pleasures to their duties, he wrote:

> But no American woman falls into the toils of matrimony as into a snare held out to her simplicity and ignorance. She has been taught beforehand what is expected of her and voluntarily and freely enters upon this engagement. She supports her new condition with courage because she chose it. . . .
>
> The same strength of purpose which the young wives of America display in bending themselves at once and without repining to the austere duties of their new condition is no less manifest in all the great trials of their lives. In no country in the world are private fortunes more precarious than in the

United States. It is not uncommon for the same man in the course of his life to rise and sink again through all the grades that lead from opulence to poverty. American women support these vicissitudes with calm and unquenchable energy; it would seem that their desires contract as easily as they expand with their fortunes.[24]

Tocqueville then observed that much of the migration to the West was by men who were in comfortable circumstances in the East.

They take their wives along with them and make them share the countless perils and privations that always attend the commencement of these expeditions. I have often met, even on the verge of the wilderness, with young women who, after having been brought up amid all the comforts of the large towns of New England, had passed, almost without any intermediate stage, from the wealthy abode of their parents to a comfortless hovel in a forest. Fever, solitude, and a tedious life had not broken the springs of their courage. Their features were impaired and faded, but their looks were firm; they appeared to be at once sad and resolute. I do not doubt that these young American women had amassed, in the education of their early years, that inward strength which they displayed under these circumstances. The early culture of the girl may still, therefore, be traced, in the United States, under the aspect of marriage; her part is changed, her habits are different, but her character is the same.[25]

This is the time when God has placed us in His world, but the issue is still the same: character.

Our foremothers faced the wilds of the wilderness; we face the wilds of moral collapse. Will we, like them, place ourselves under the authority of God's Word so that our great-great-granddaughters will be as encouraged and inspired by our example as we are by theirs?

I believe that Christian women are weary of fluff. They are ready to sacrifice their pleasure for their Christian duty. They have an increasing awareness that the way of duty is the way of true safety. They have a growing realization that their love for Christ grows exponentially with their knowledge of Him. They are yearning to have truth pressed into their minds and hearts because they, too, cry out with Elizabeth Prentiss:

> *More love to Thee, O Christ, More love to Thee!*
> *Hear Thou the prayer I make On bended knee;*
> *This is my earnest plea:*
> *More love, O Christ, to Thee!*
> *More love to Thee,*
> *More love to Thee!*

> *Once earthly joy I craved, Sought peace and rest;*
> *Now Thee alone I seek—Give what is best;*
> *This all my prayer shall be:*
> *More love, O Christ, to Thee!*
> *More love to Thee,*
> *More love to Thee!*

> *Then shall my latest breath Whisper Thy praise;*
> *This be the parting cry My heart shall raise;*
> *This still its prayer shall be:*
> *More love, O Christ, to Thee!*
> *More love to Thee,*
> *More love to Thee!*

IN SUMMARY

The true woman's rule for faith and practice is God's Word. So being a true woman today means standing against the cultural paradigm. A true reflection of redemption in our time demands critical thinking. The true woman must push everything through the grid of God's Word. She must develop a biblical apologetic, or explanation, for every aspect of her life. She must think theologically in order to live faithfully. There is no room for carelessness.

The true woman will theologize rather than psychologize her life. Three basic theological themes will be woven through this book. Obviously there are many others, but these, I think, form the bedrock for being a true woman: the sovereignty of God, the covenant of grace, and redemption.

Personal Reflection

1. Select specific Scriptures to pray for various people. Write these in your journal and memorize them. For example, I pray Ephesians 3:14-19 for my family.

2. In your journal, write a statement of your life purpose, including your standard to help you determine how to fulfill that purpose.

3. Read two or three sections of Psalm 119 each day and meditate on the excellency of God's Word. Select some of these verses to memorize and to pray.

4. Write a statement of your worldview. If you have never thought about this and have difficulty formulating it, just write that. You will be asked to do this again at the end of this book. It will be interesting to compare the two.

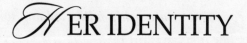

PART TWO

HER IDENTITY

What identifies the true woman?

What are the results of this identity?

❧

MY PRAYER

*That you will have a richer understanding
of our covenant relationship with God and with one
another, and that you will have a deep desire to reflect
your redemption in all of life.*

❧

MY CHALLENGE

*"Therefore, [sisters], since we have confidence
to enter the Most Holy Place by the blood of Jesus . . . Let
us hold unswervingly to the hope we profess, for he who
promised is faithful. And let us consider how we may
spur one another on toward love and good deeds. Let
us not give up meeting together, as some are in
the habit of doing, but let us encourage
one another. . . ."*

— HEBREWS 10:19, 23-25

❧

*R*EBELLIOUS ADULT CHILD

The long distance phone call received that bleak afternoon in December seemed life-shattering. "There is a couple in our church on the verge of separating," the caller reported. "The husband is an alcoholic and on drugs. That man is your son!" What a shock! We knew that George had not been as interested in spiritual things as we would have liked, but he was still attending church. We had no idea the situation had deteriorated so, and we were devastated. Later we found that things were not as bad as reported, but they still were not good. We began to realize that although he had conformed outwardly in many ways even during teen and college years, there was much inner rebellion in spiritual matters. And now his life was a wreck, his marriage in shambles, and he didn't seem to care.

At first my deep inner pain was life-consuming, and the situation occupied my thoughts day and night. But as always, when I looked to the Lord and His Word, the promises began to jump off the pages of Scripture day after day, comforting my troubled heart. "Why are you downcast, O my soul? Why so disturbed within me? Put your hope in God, for I will yet praise him, my Savior and my God" (Psalm 42:5).

The sovereignty of God became an even more precious doctrine than it had been. How comforting was Proverbs 21:30: "There is no wisdom, no insight, no plan that can succeed against the Lord."

But the clincher verse that sustained me month after month, as I claimed its covenantal promise, was Isaiah 59:21: "'As for me, this is my covenant with them,' says the Lord. 'My Spirit, who is on you, and my words that I have put in your mouth will not depart from your mouth, or from the mouths of your children, or from the mouths of their descendants from this time on and forever,' says the Lord."

We were able to develop a network of prayer for him that literally extended around the world. Missionary friends and members in our local church joined with us in asking God for His mercy.

The Lord performed a miracle slowly and gradually over a couple of years. Very soon George was in deep agony over his situation and the loss of his family. He later said that during all those rebellious years, he had always prayed, "God, don't give up on me." God put George flat on his face, but He did not give up on him.

My husband and I were encouraged as George gradually opened up to us more and more. At each opportunity we shared Scripture and sent books and tapes, which he eagerly received. Almost daily the long distance phone calls were discipling opportunities. He began to see that the Lord was his only help and reached out for the salvation that God alone could provide.

Now, six years later, he is a growing Christian, a deacon in the church, and faithfully instructing his children in the Word of God. The marriage is not yet restored, but the last chapter in this story has not yet been lived or written.

—*Name withheld*

✐ RECIPIENT
OF REDEMPTION

*The conduct of Jesus Christ towards the female sex was one
of the most attractive excellences of his beautiful character,
though perhaps it is one of the least noticed. To him they
must ever point, as not only the Saviour of their souls, but
as the advocate of their rights and the guardian of their peace.*

Female Piety

As a redeemed daughter of the King of kings, the Christian
woman has a new identity. Her identity is not determined
by her situation nor by her relationships with men, as feminists
believe we are saying, but by her Savior. Her concern is not self-
image but being an image-bearer of the Lord God.

In the last chapter I gave a catalog of conversations. Most of
these represent many conversations with many women. I don't
mean to sound callous, but these women had unknowingly
embraced the cultural idols of our day: fun, self-indulgence, self-
fulfillment, and materialism. They bought the lies: You're worth it;
you can have it all; look out for number one.

The uncomfortable truth is that even though we say we have
a Christocentric worldview, when the pressure is on, we often shift
to an egocentric view of our situation. We think selfishly rather
than redemptively.

Woman's nurturing strengths generally give us a greater
propensity to emotion and sensitivity. Perhaps this is part of the

reason that women often appear more receptive to the Gospel, as the nineteenth-century preacher noted:

> . . . look into our congregations and churches, and see how largely they are composed of females. How many more of their sex, than of the other, avail themselves of the offer of gospel mercy, and come under the influence of religion. It is in the female bosom, however we may account for the fact, that piety finds a home on earth. The door of woman's heart is often thrown wide open to receive the Divine guest, when man refuses Him an entrance. And it is by thus yielding to the power of godliness, and reflecting upon others the beauties of holiness, that she maintains her standing and her influence in society.[1]

But this female strength will become a destructive weakness if our faith is based solely on feeling and excitement rather than on God's truth. Our experience should be the response to truth rather than the determiner of truth.

Remember, the true woman's standard is God's Word. In *The Micah Mandate*, George Grant gives a riveting quote from Eadburgh, a princess in seventh-century England who was known for her holy life and good deeds among the poor:

> We do the lost and lonely, the desperate and deprived no favors by offering them anything less than the offense of the Gospel. There is no tenderness of heart, no sensitivity of soul, no generosity of spirit in accommodating men's sin in this life when the consequences be so dire in the next. Let us therefore hold firmly to this just cause, let us therefore raise up this just banner: His Word alone. In this fashion do we fulfill what the Lord requires: but to do justly.[2]

We do ourselves and others no favors by rationalizing or trivializing sin, or by psychologizing or marginalizing the Gospel. We must valiantly "raise up this just banner: His Word alone."

Without a thorough understanding of God's sovereign redemptive grace, we will slip into a performance-based mentality that propels the pendulum of our lives toward the frustration of legalism or the looseness of liberalism. Without a grip on grace, we will be form without substance.

Twenty-five years ago I met each week with two other young women, and we studied the doctrines of grace. There were days when they would ask me, "Why do we need to know all of this?" I wasn't sure, but I knew we needed to dig deep into God's Word, and I didn't want to do it alone. A couple of years later, one of the women was diagnosed with cancer. I will never forget her letter to me in the final days of her life: "Now I know why we had to do that study." She went on to tell me that knowing those truths gave her the sturdy faith she needed to face death and deal with leaving a husband and four children.

In this chapter we will look briefly at the three theological themes woven throughout this book: God's sovereignty, the covenant of grace, and redemption. In the classic work *Redemption Accomplished and Applied*, John Murray wrote:

> On so great a theme as Christ's redemptive accomplishment I am profoundly conscious of the limitations that encompass our attempts at exposition. Thought and expression stagger in the presence of the spectacle that confronts us in the vicarious sin-bearing of the Lord of glory. Here we must realize that we are dealing with the mystery of godliness, and eternity will not reach the bottom of it nor exhaust its praise. Yet it is ours to proclaim it and continue the attempt to expound and defend its truth.[3]

John Murray was an esteemed professor of systematic theology at Westminster Seminary. If he was conscious of his limitations in discussing "so great a theme" as he set out to write an entire book on the subject, you can imagine how I feel. But my prayer is that this summary will whet your appetite to dig deeper into these glorious truths and that you will be wonder-struck at how "wide and long and high and deep is the love of Christ, and to know this love that surpasses knowledge—that you may be filled to the measure of all the fullness of God" (Ephesians 3:18-19).

GOD'S SOVEREIGNTY

I love to hear R. C. Sproul talk. His inimitable style and his brilliant intellect are stimulating, but it is his sheer delight in the sovereignty of God that is so engaging. A typical "Sproulism" is: "If there is one maverick molecule in all the universe, then God is not sovereign. And if God is not sovereign, He is not God."

That pretty much says it all.

God is sovereign in creation, in providence, and in salvation. He is omnipotent, omnipresent, and omniscient. He is King of kings, Lord of lords. His holiness and majesty are unmatched.

John Calvin was the theologian of the Reformation. He systematized and articulated the truths of the Bible that were rediscovered in the Reformation revival. Sproul says of Calvin, "Reading Calvin at times is like reading lyric poetry. The majesty of his language was appropriate to the loftiness of the subjects he treated. He was a man intoxicated by the majesty of God. No theologian, before or since, had such a grasp of His beauty and loveliness. This marks everything that Calvin wrote and did."[4]

It certainly marks these words from Calvin's pen:

> . . . man is never sufficiently touched and affected by the awareness of his lowly state until he has compared himself with God's majesty. . . . we see how Abraham recognizes more clearly that he is earth and dust (Genesis 18:27) when once he had come nearer to beholding God's glory; and how Elijah, with uncovered face, cannot bear to await his approach, such is the awesomeness of his appearance (1 Kings 19:13). And what can man do, who is rottenness itself (Job 13:28) and a worm (Job 7:5; Psalm 22:6), when even the very cherubim

must veil their faces out of fear (Isaiah 6:2)? It is this indeed of which the prophet Isaiah speaks: "The sun will blush and the moon be confounded when the Lord of Hosts shall reign"(Isaiah 24:23); that is, when he shall bring forth his splendor and cause it to draw nearer, the brightest thing will become darkness before it (Isaiah 2:10, 19).[5]

God's sovereignty is the glorious musical accompaniment that plays throughout the biblical drama. At times the music is barely audible, and at times it breaks forth in a stirring crescendo. But it is always there.

God is sovereign in *creation*.

God's sovereignty in creation is challenged by the ridiculous theory of evolution, but is celebrated by the psalmist:

> *Come, let us sing for joy to the Lord; . . .*
>   *For the Lord is the great God,*
>   *the great King above all gods.*
> *In his hand are the depths of the earth,*
>   *and the mountain peaks belong to him.*
> *The sea is his, for he made it,*
>   *and his hands formed the dry land.*
> *Come, let us bow down in worship,*
>   *let us kneel before the Lord our Maker;*
>   *for he is our God*
> *and we are the people of his pasture,*
>   *the flock under his care.*
>   *— Psalm 95:1, 3-7*

Our view of creation affects our view of life. If I began as the result of chaotic chance, then chaos is the journey and destination of life. The knowledge of God's sovereign purpose and design of creation injects massive doses of purpose, design, and significance into every moment of my existence.

God is sovereign in *providence*.

Providence means to think about, care or prepare for, in advance.

The Westminster Shorter Catechism says: "God's works of providence are his most holy, wise, and powerful preserving and governing of all his creatures and all their actions."[6]

Calvin wrote: " . . . let my readers grasp that providence means not that by which God idly observes from heaven what takes place on earth, but that by which, as keeper of the keys, he governs all events."[7]

Calvin further noted that this doctrine has profound practical implications:

> . . . he has surely benefited greatly who has so learned to meditate upon God's providence that he can always recall his mind to this point: the Lord has willed it; therefore it must be borne, not only because one may not contend against it, but also because he wills nothing but what is just and expedient. To sum this up: when we are unjustly wounded by men, let us overlook their wickedness (which would but worsen our pain and sharpen our minds to revenge), remember to mount up to God, and learn to believe for certain that whatever our enemy has wickedly committed against us was permitted and sent by God's just dispensation.[8]

This advice is quite different from the introspective psychobabble we hear today. This biblical view sees more than the immediate circumstance. This is a big-picture perspective that believes that God's good providence has willed it; therefore, it is just and expedient.

Joseph had this perspective and succinctly stated it to his terrified brothers: "You intended to harm me, but God intended it for good to accomplish what is now being done, the saving of many lives" (Genesis 50:20).

These men who had sold him into slavery were now sprawled out before him exclaiming, "We are your slaves!"

Joseph did not excuse his brothers' sin, but he could explain

it. God's mighty hand of providence had been at work maneu-
vering events to use Joseph eventually to provide food for His
people. So Joseph could be forgiving rather than bitter. He
responded, "'So then, don't be afraid. I will provide for you and
your children.' And he reassured them and spoke kindly to them"
(Genesis 50:21).

The Old Testament is full of dramatic instances of the hand of
God at work: the parting of the Red Sea, the walls of Jericho
falling down without a single Israelite touching a stone, three men
emerging from a fiery furnace without even the smell of smoke on
their clothes. But Joseph, like most other Old Testament believers,
lived through the dailiness of life without these epic experiences.
Joseph was abused by his brothers, falsely accused by his boss's
wife, and misused by a fellow prisoner. But he clung to his knowledge about the character of God, and that shaped his own
character.

Luck and chance are pagan words that have no place in the
believer's vocabulary. They are an assault on the sovereign providence of God.

God is sovereign in *salvation*.

God's sovereignty in creation and providence are magnificent,
but His sovereignty in our salvation is surely the zenith of His love.
Paul expressed this in his doxology to God's grace:

> *Praise be to the God and Father of our Lord Jesus Christ, who
> has blessed us in the heavenly realms with every spiritual
> blessing in Christ. For he chose us in him before the creation of
> the world to be holy and blameless in his sight. In love he pre-
> destined us to be adopted as his sons through Jesus Christ, in
> accordance with his pleasure and will — to the praise of his glo-
> rious grace, which he has freely given us in the One he loves.*
> — *Ephesians 1:3-6*

If we do anything to merit salvation, then it is no longer grace.
Even saying, "I chose Christ," denies His claims that "You did not

choose me, but I chose you. . . . " (John 15:16), and "No one can come to me unless the Father who sent me draws him" (John 6:44).

If I am the initiator in my salvation, if I chose Christ, then I am ultimately responsible for my salvation and therefore should receive at least part of the glory. As Calvin said, "If even the least ability came from ourselves, we would also have some share of the merit. . . . not a whit remains to man to glory in, for the whole of salvation comes from God."[9]

Charles Haddon Spurgeon, the "Prince of Preachers," in a sermon entitled "Divine Sovereignty," said:

> There is no attribute of God more comforting to His children than the doctrine of Divine Sovereignty. . . . There is nothing for which the children of God ought more earnestly to contend than . . . the kingship of God over all the works of His own hands. . . .
>
> On the other hand, there is no doctrine more hated by worldlings . . . as the great, stupendous, but yet most certain doctrine of the Sovereignty of the infinite Jehovah. Men will allow God to be everywhere except upon His throne . . . when God ascends His throne, His creatures then gnash their teeth; and when we proclaim an enthroned God, and His right to do as He wills with His own, to dispose of His creatures as He thinks well, without consulting them in the matter, then it is that . . . men turn a deaf ear to us, for God on His throne is not the God they love. They love Him anywhere better than they do when He sits with His sceptre in His hand and His crown upon His head. But it is God upon the throne that we love to preach. It is God upon His throne whom we trust.[10]

Any inclination to deny such a glorious and gracious truth is simply an attempt to exalt self. It is not until we come to the end of ourselves that we can even begin to apprehend the magnitude and the victory of God's sovereign love for us.

Moses did not mince words when he told the Israelites:

For you are a people holy to the Lord your God. The Lord your God has chosen you out of all the peoples on the face of the earth to be his people, his treasured possession. The Lord did not set his affection on you and choose you because you were more numerous than other peoples, for you were the fewest of all peoples. But it was because the Lord loved you and kept the oath he swore to your forefathers that he brought you out with a mighty hand and redeemed you from the land of slavery. . . .
                                            — *Deuteronomy 7:6-8*

Peter echoed Moses' words when he wrote: "But you are a chosen people, a royal priesthood, a holy nation, a people belonging to God, that you may declare the praises of him who called you out of darkness into his wonderful light. Once you were not a people, but now you are the people of God; once you had not received mercy, but now you have received mercy" (1 Peter 2:9-10).

Some may ask why God chose some and not others. But perhaps the better question is: Why did He choose me? Why would He set His affection on me and make me His treasured possession? There is no reasonable explanation except that "He loved me. . . . " No wonder Paul erupted into such passionate praise in writing to Timothy: "The grace of our Lord was poured out on me abundantly, along with the faith and love that are in Christ Jesus. . . . I was shown mercy so that in me, the worst of sinners, Christ Jesus might display his unlimited patience as an example for those who would believe on him and receive eternal life. Now to the King eternal, immortal, invisible, the only God, be honor and glory for ever and ever. Amen" (1 Timothy 1:14-17).

God reveals Himself to us in His Word as a sovereign God of glory. His sovereignty in creation, providence, and salvation form the bedrock of our worldview. His sovereignty is our hope and our joy. It is the knowledge of His sovereign reign over the world and our lives that makes sense out of what often looks and feels like chaos.

I met Melissa Roop during lunch at a women's retreat. I was immediately drawn to this delightful woman who had a charming way of enfolding everyone at the table into the group. When the woman next to me whispered, "Melissa's son has cancer," I knew Melissa was not form without substance. Later when I talked with her, she said with a clear voice and steady eyes, "God is sovereign. Whatever He does is good and right. I trust Him." This was faith, not fatalism. It was neither easy nor painless, but when the crisis came, Melissa's unambiguous worldview kicked in. Melissa's faith was rooted in a sovereign God of love. Her view of Him came from His Word and not from her feelings.

When we manufacture our own perception of God, we build an idol. When we bring Him to the confines of our experience (my God would never do this), we reduce Him to our level. And that is terrifying. The only God it makes sense to entrust ourselves to is the God of the Bible.

Of course, this raises questions. It is a mystery that we cannot fully comprehend with our finite minds. The balance between human responsibility and divine sovereignty is difficult to distinguish. But as King Nebuchadnezzar dramatically learned, whether we can understand it or not, God is sovereign.

Nebuchadnezzar's greatness extended to "the distant parts of the earth." One day as he walked on the roof of his royal palace, he boasted, "'Is not this the great Babylon I have built as the royal residence, by my mighty power and for the glory of my majesty?'

"The words were still on his lips when a voice came from heaven, 'This is what is decreed for you, King Nebuchadnezzar: Your royal authority has been taken from you. You will be driven away from people and will live with the wild animals. . . . until you acknowledge that the Most High is sovereign over the kingdoms of men and gives them to anyone he wishes.'"

And that is exactly what happened.

We are often as independent and prideful as Nebuchadnezzar. May it not take such drastic means to bring us to our sanity. Nebuchadnezzar finally raised his eyes toward heaven. May we do the same.

At the end of that time, I, Nebuchadnezzar, raised my eyes toward heaven, and my sanity was restored. Then I praised the Most High; I honored and glorified him who lives forever.

His dominion is an eternal dominion; his kingdom endures from generation to generation. All the peoples of the earth are regarded as nothing. He does as he pleases with the powers of heaven and the peoples of the earth. No one can hold back his hand or say to him: "What have you done?"

— Daniel 4

God's sovereignty is the background music on every page of Scripture and on every page of my life. I marvel at my friends who are trained musicians. They detect sounds that my untrained ear does not hear. I may never learn to hear the musical sounds they do, but I can learn to detect the sweet strains of God's sovereignty in my life.

THE COVENANT OF GRACE

A covenant is a binding agreement. Grace is God's lovingkindness that we do not deserve.

The arrangement whereby we relate to God is called covenant. That arrangement requires sinlessness because God is perfect, and He will have no fellowship with sin.

When God created human beings, He entered into a covenant of works with them, thus elevating man and woman to a position of fellowship with Himself. This was possible because Adam and Eve were sinless. God could have created puppets, but He didn't. God gave Adam and Eve the ability to obey or to disobey—to remain sinless or to sin. They chose to sin.

The truth that the Creator of the universe was willing to live in fellowship with the creatures of His hand is too glorious to comprehend. What is even more amazing is that when the creatures did not keep their part of the covenant, the Creator already had a better plan. He was still willing to live in fellowship with His people, and He was even willing to provide the way. This is what is known as the covenant of grace.

Sin had to be punished because the requirement to live in fellowship with God was the same: sinlessness. God met that demand by doing for us what we could not do for ourselves. God gave His own Son as the perfect sacrifice for the sins of His people. Jesus met the demands of the covenant, and we are the beneficiaries. This is grace. When we respond in repentance and faith, we enter into a covenant relationship with the Lord God. It is now our privilege and responsibility to obey Him from a heart of love. And the glorious truth that must be emphasized is that we can live a life of loving obedience because of what Jesus accomplished on the cross and because of what He is doing in our lives through the power of His Holy Spirit.

The covenant encompasses all that God is to us and all that He has done for us. It encapsulates all that is involved in our relationship with Him. It is the unifying concept in the Bible. It is the thread that ties all of Scripture together. Unless we see this thread, we will view Scripture as a series of disconnected, disjointed stories and events; and the effect will be that our lives will tend to be disconnected and disjointed.

Think back to that dramatic moment in the Garden after Adam and Eve had sinned. They were preposterously dressed in leaves and hiding behind a bush. But God came, and "the Lord God called to the man" (Genesis 3:9). Then after pronouncing the curse and the remedy, "the Lord God made garments of skin for Adam and his wife and clothed them" (Genesis 3:21).

Here is the essence of the covenant: God came, He called, and He clothed. And He has been doing the same down through the ages. He comes to us, He calls us to Himself, and He clothes us with the righteousness of Christ. He relates to us not on the basis of our performance, but on the basis of His provision.

Paul Kooistra, former president of Covenant Theological Seminary, wrote:

This is no ordinary relationship! Casually held, regularly broken human contracts surround us, often victimize us in our world. The divine covenant stands out in brilliant contrast. God chose to bind Himself eternally to His people in utterly faithful love. To our faith-fathers He revealed Himself—to Adam, Noah, Abraham, Moses, David. The essence of His declaration: I will be your God, and you will be my people. I will dwell with you. The Holy Scripture permanently records God's unfolding covenant with His people. The promise comes to fullest expression in Jesus, who is Immanuel—God with us![11]

His promise that He will be our God and that we will be His people runs from Genesis to Revelation. God said to Abraham, "I will establish my covenant as an everlasting covenant between me and you and your descendants after you for the generations to come, to be your God and the God of your descendants after you" (Genesis 17:7).

And in the book of Revelation we read:

Then I saw a new heaven and a new earth, for the first heaven and the first earth had passed away. . . . I saw the Holy City, the new Jerusalem, coming down out of heaven from God, prepared as a bride beautifully dressed for her husband. And I heard a loud voice from the throne saying, "Now the dwelling of God is with men, and he will live with them. They will be his people, and God himself will be with them and be their God. He will wipe every tear from their eyes. There will be no more death or mourning or crying or pain, for the old order of things has passed away." He who was seated on the throne said, "I am making everything new!" Then he said, "Write this down, for these words are trustworthy and true."

— Revelation 21:1-5

He is our God—this is our hope.

We are His people—this is our identity.

He lives among us—this is our joy.

These words are trustworthy and true—this is our assurance.

REDEMPTION

The dictionary defines redemption as a recovery of something pawned or mortgaged, deliverance upon payment of a ransom, a rescue. To redeem is to recover ownership by paying a specified sum. This presupposes bondage or captivity.

Israel's captivity in Egypt vividly illustrates our bondage in sin. Their deliverance out of this slavery foreshadows our deliverance from sin. Jesus said, "I tell you the truth, everyone who sins is a slave to sin" (John 8:34). He then offered the freedom that only He can give: "So if the Son sets you free, you will be free indeed" (John 8:36).

Sin and slavery are not fashionable topics today. There is so much emphasis on self-image, self-esteem, self-worth, and self-actualization that talk of the total depravity and enslavement of the unredeemed sinner is most unpopular. A few years ago I was teaching the children in our church Romans 3:23: "for all have sinned and fall short of the glory of God." A mother came and told me that she didn't want her daughter hearing such negative messages. She feared it would damage her self-worth. She contended that I should just talk about God's love. I tried to explain that we cannot understand the enormity of God's love without understanding the extent of our sin. Rather than risk her child's "emotional health," she left the church. The sad reality is that the world is playing psychological games with our minds with this emphasis on self.

The title of John Murray's classic work on this subject crystallizes the biblical concept. *Redemption Accomplished and Applied*— what a strong, triumphant statement! Our redemption is not a possibility. It is an accomplished fact. Our redemption has been accomplished by the finished work of Christ upon the cross. It is applied to His children by His Spirit when He draws them to Himself.

Murray wrote: "The language of redemption is the language of purchase and more specifically of ransom. And ransom is the securing of a release by the payment of a price. . . . Redemption applies to every respect in which we are bound, and it releases us unto a liberty that is nothing less than the liberty of the glory of the children of God."[12]

Jesus is the Redeemer. His very life and death were the redemption price. He paid in full. We are redeemed!

It is no wonder that Paul continues his doxology to God's grace: "In him we have redemption through his blood, the forgiveness of sins, in accordance with the riches of God's grace that he lavished on us with all wisdom and understanding" (Ephesians 1:7-8).

History is the story of redemption. This story is much bigger than I. I am not the main character in the drama of redemption. I am not the point. But by God's grace I am a part of it. My subplot is integral to the whole. It is far more significant to have a small part in this story than to star in my own puny production. This is a cosmic story that will run throughout eternity. Will I play my part with grace and joy, or will I go for the short-run, insignificant story that really has no point? This was the core issue facing the women whose conversations I recorded in chapter 2. Would they think redemptively, or would they think selfishly? Would they see their situations in light of the big picture of redemption, or would they focus only on their personal pain or inconvenience?

In *My Utmost for His Highest*, Oswald Chambers wrote: "The feebleness of the churches is being criticized today, and the criticism is justified. One reason for the feebleness is that there has not been this concentration of spiritual energy; we have not brooded enough on the tragedy of Calvary or on the meaning of Redemption."[13]

Brood with me on the tragedy of Calvary and the meaning of redemption. The following quote from John Murray is one I return to often when I am tempted to be feeble in my faith:

Our sins have separated us from God.... there was only one, and there will not need to be another, who bore the full weight of the divine judgment upon sin and bore it so as to end it. The lost will eternally suffer in the satisfaction of justice. But they will never satisfy it. Christ satisfied justice. "The Lord hath laid on him the iniquity of us all" (Isaiah 53:6). He was made sin and he was made a curse. He bore our iniquities. He bore the unrelieved and unmitigated damnation of sin, and he finished it. That is the spectacle that confronts us in Gethsemane and on Calvary. This is the explanation of Gethsemane with its bloody sweat and agonizing cry, "O my Father, if it be possible, let this cup pass from me" (Matthew 26:39). And this is the explanation of the most mysterious utterance that ever ascended from earth to heaven, "My God, my God, why hast thou forsaken me?" ... the most solemn spectacle in all history, a spectacle unparalleled, unique, unrepeated, and unrepeatable.... Here we are the spectators of a wonder the praise and glory of which eternity will not exhaust. It is the Lord of glory, the Son of God incarnate, the God-man, drinking the cup given him by the eternal Father, the cup of woe and of indescribable agony. We almost hesitate to say so. But it must be said. It is God in our nature forsaken of God. ... There is no reproduction or parallel in the experience of archangels or of the greatest saints. The faintest parallel would crush the holiest of men and the mightiest of the angelic host....

It is the spectacle of Gethsemane and Calvary, thus interpreted, that opens to us the folds of unspeakable love. The Father did not spare his own Son. He spared nothing that the dictates of unrelenting rectitude demanded. And it is the undercurrent of the Son's acquiescence that we hear when he said, "Nevertheless not my will, but thine, be done" (Luke 22:42). It was in order that eternal and invincible love might find the full realization of its urge and purpose in redemption by price and by power.... It is the same love manifested in the mystery of Gethsemane's agony and of Calvary's accursed tree that wraps eternal security around the people of God....

"He that spared not his own Son, but delivered him up for us all, how shall he not with him also freely give us all things? . . ."

"Who shall separate us from the love of Christ? Shall tribulation, or distress, or persecution, or famine, or nakedness, or peril, or sword? . . ."

"For I am persuaded that neither death nor life nor angels nor principalities nor things present nor things to come nor powers nor height nor depth nor any other creature will be able to separate us from the love of God which is in Christ Jesus our Lord" (Romans 8:32, 35, 38-39).

That is the security which a perfect atonement secures and it is the perfection of the atonement that secures it.[14]

IN SUMMARY

The true woman is a recipient of redemption. God set His sovereign affection upon her. He bound Himself to her in covenant faithfulness to be her God. He has redeemed her with His own blood. She is His treasured possession.

"And the Lord has declared this day that you are his people, his treasured possession as he promised, and that you are to keep all his commands. He has declared that he will set you in praise, fame and honor high above all the nations he has made and that you will be a people holy to the Lord your God, as he promised" (Deuteronomy 26:18).

The folds of unspeakable love . . . a love that wraps eternal security around us . . . because we are His treasured possessions.

This is the indisputable identity of the true woman.

Personal Reflection

1. How do you define yourself? Meditate on the fact that you are God's treasured possession. Write a prayer in your journal thanking Him that your identity is in Him.

2. Read Ephesians 1 every day for a week.

3. Write your own doxology of praise to the Lord in your journal.

4. What circumstance are you currently living through? Meditate on God's sovereign providence and ask Him to help you hear the music of His sovereignty on this page of your life.

5. Read Matthew 10:29-31 and thank God that He is aware of and cares about the most minute detail of your life.

$\mathscr{R}$ APED

On August 10, 1988, I became a statistic—one of thousands of women raped in the country that year. I also became part of another statistic, a smaller, much rarer group of women: I became pregnant as a result of that tragic event. When this realization bolted like lightning out of the depths of impossibility and into my life, nothing was ever again the same.

Mary, the mother of Jesus, is my kindred sister, for not only is she redeemed by the atoning work of her Son on the cross—and thus my kin, but I feel an affinity for Mary in the similarity of our experiences. As an unmarried, pregnant young woman facing the unexpected, the unasked for, and the seemingly uncharted course before her, how did she handle it? Was she as frightened as I was? Did her mind flood with questions, an endless stream of thoughts, day and night, through leisure and labor, whether in a crowd or alone? How was it possible? Why has this happened? What will I do now?

Where lay Mary's comfort? "Let it be to me according to your word" (Luke 1:38). This was no accidental pregnancy. It might have been unexpected to her, but it was part of an eternal plan that had its roots in the unchangeable Word of God. Perhaps Mary had been like many betrothed young girls, daydreaming about the life she would have with Joseph, the household they would build, the children they would raise and love. That is, until this day when the greatest inconvenience to her dreams became the reality instead.

She discovered suddenly that her plans had no substance, held no meaning, outside of the providence of God. They were wisps of dreams that scattered in the tumult of this storm. Every thought of Joseph, a home full of children, or a place in the community was etched with the specter of this incredible news. Mary now dared not even consider that the plans for the rest of this very day were sure to come about, only that God's Word was reliable.

She knew that the lives of the saints had been directed in extraordinary ways to bring about God's will, but Mary had likely perceived herself to be among those whose paths were relatively undisturbed by the supernatural. She was no Sarah—wife, mother, and grandmother to the patriarchs; nor was she an Esther sent by God into the royal court of the enemy of Israel. These were the heroines of the faith; she was demure, frightened, ordinary Mary.

This was impossibility reined in by a purposeful God. Its only sane explanation lay in His perfect, yet secret, will. For whatever reason, she had been chosen particularly for this task. God in His wisdom altered her life and not another's. God in His goodness would also sustain her with grace and peace.

Once the angel made his announcement, he departed from her, and she was left to face her family and friends alone. Nonetheless, undaunted, sure of God's grace, and glowing with humility for being chosen, she hurried to visit her cousin Elizabeth, whom the angel said had also conceived a child, John, who would be the Baptizer. As she approached the older woman, her presence caused the baby in Elizabeth's womb to leap. Not a word was spoken, but the hand of the Lord had already reached out to cause Elizabeth to be filled with the Holy Spirit and joyful about the news. To guarantee a second witness to verify Mary's account, God sent an angel to inform Joseph of His plans. There was no stone left unturned.

Mary didn't miss a single thing. She observed and listened and obeyed and pondered it all in her heart, and she witnessed a world captured by the sovereign hand of God controlling everything from the greatest happenings to the most minute details. But what does Mary's confidence in a sovereign God mean to me? Though her situation seemed difficult, it was actually very good. My trials, on the other hand, were difficult, and they were instigated by evil—something that had no place in Mary's situation.

"And we know that all things work together for good to those who love God, to those who are the called according to His purposes" (Romans 8:28). My comfort, like Mary's, is in the Word of God. There is nothing that is not good that comes into the lives of God's own. Once my vision of how I thought my life should be was shattered, the clearer, sharper, more beautiful picture of God's perfect and reliable plan came into focus. There's nothing—no convenience, no dream come true—I would have traded for that.

The speculative whispers and wagging tongues were more often audible than not, and not every raised eyebrow could be hidden behind a church bulletin. Believing friends fell away, unsure of what to say to me, and the looks of complete strangers traveled from my growing midsection to my empty ring finger and settled on my face, bursting with unspoken curiosity; but my security rested not in the approval of this generation.

This world considers any disruption of its thoroughly detailed preparation for a life of convenience a rational excuse for unbridled anguish and rebellion. To most people, the thankful prayer I raise to God every morning for the radical explosion that took place in my life seven years ago seems akin to insanity. My child's birth will never impact the world the way the incarnation of the very Son of God has—and it would be blasphemous to assume any more similarity between the two stories than I have dared here. But the disruptions in the plans of Mary and me served to bring both of us to the same conclusion: Sometimes God's purpose in shattering the peace in our lives is to remind us that He has a purpose for everything. Consequently, my confidence in His sovereignty may at times be nudged, but it will never be shaken. Though I may anguish over future trials, I will not have to search for the antidote to my sorrow, for I have laid my faith on the foundation of God's undeniable goodness.

And see how very good He is to me by adding blessing upon

blessing—a beautiful child to raise up in the knowledge of God's amazing providence. "Don't ask God for patience; you might get your prayers answered" goes the popular warning. I say, "Don't pray for a life of convenience; you might get it—and wouldn't that be too bad?"*

—Name withheld

---

*Used by permission from <i>Tabletalk</i>, December 1995,
Ligonier Ministries, Orlando, Florida.

$\mathcal{A}$ REFLECTION
OF REDEMPTION

*Christian women, you must be the brightest patterns of
kindness and mercy which our selfish world contains,
and add to temperance, patience, and godliness,
Christian kindness and charity. Such a character cannot
be unnoticed or unacknowledged. . . .*

Female Piety

T he redeemed are to reflect the image of the Redeemer. Neither
syrupy sweetness nor tearful testimonies are a true reflection
of redemption.

A true reflection demands the hard stuff of repentance, faith,
obedience, and forgiveness. These are not one-time events; they
are lifelong processes. To reflect redemption, the true woman must
grab the promises of God and integrate them into every aspect of
her life.

In short, this is the process of sanctification: " . . . the work of
God's free grace, whereby we are renewed in the whole man after
the image of God, and are enabled more and more to die unto sin,
and live unto righteousness."[1]

When I was young, I used to hear it said sometimes that
someone was so heavenly minded they were no earthly good. I
don't hear that anymore. I'm glad I don't, because it didn't
make sense then, and it doesn't make sense now. As George
Grant has said:

We cannot be authentically Christian and simultaneously be so heavenly-minded that we're no earthly good any more than we can be so earthly-minded that we're no heavenly good. The only possibility for us is to be so heavenly-minded that we do the earth good. And that demands a substantive lifestyle balance where both faith and work are operative, where both holiness and service motivate, where both Word and deed dominate, where the Gospel is proclaimed in both doctrine and life.[2]

A pilgrim perspective helps give this balance.

A PILGRIM PERSPECTIVE

Even when I have intellectually embraced a biblical worldview, the work of maintaining this perspective is unceasing. I easily become comfortable in and attached to this world. I am often captivated by its charms. Our two oldest grandchildren unknowingly gave me a vivid example that helps me stay on course.

During the Christmas holidays Hunter, age six, and Mary Kate, age four, spent a night with us. We went out to eat, bought Christmas presents for their mom and dad, and visited a live Nativity scene. On the way home Gene drove through a neighborhood to show us the Christmas decorations. The homes were palatial and the decorations elaborate. I was quite dazzled. Then I became aware of the conversation in the back seat. "Our mansion is bigger than these." The reply: "If you connected all these mansions together, ours is still bigger." I was curious. You would be hard-pressed to call their home a mansion. In fact, you would have to "connect" several houses like theirs to equal the houses we were seeing.

"Our mansion is more beautiful than these," I heard one of them say.

"What mansion are you talking about?" I asked.

"Our mansion in heaven," they responded, surprised that I even had to ask.

Hunter and Mary Kate were unimpressed with the sights and lights because they knew with a childlike simplicity that what they possess is far grander. They are simply pilgrims passing through.

The psalmist knew this too.

A PILGRIM PSALM

Psalm 84 was probably written by a Levite who normally functioned in the temple service but was unable to go to Jerusalem. This may have been in the time that Sennacherib was ravaging Judah. Whatever the reason, the psalmist begins by expressing his longing for God's presence.

How lovely is your dwelling place, O Lord Almighty! My soul yearns, even faints, for the courts of the Lord; my heart and my flesh cry out for the living God.

It is not difficult to imagine the psalmist's attachment to the temple. Remember, when the Israelites left Egypt, God led them through the wilderness with a pillar of cloud by day and a pillar of fire by night. This was a visible evidence of His presence with them. At Sinai God gave Moses explicit instructions for building the tabernacle. Moses obediently followed these instructions, and when the work was completed, "the cloud covered the Tent of Meeting, and the glory of the Lord filled the tabernacle" (Exodus 40:34). The tabernacle stood in the center of the Israelite community with the various tribes surrounding it. Here is a dramatic manifestation of God's covenant promise: I will be your God; you will be My people; I will dwell among you.

When Israel was settled in the promised land, Solomon was given the assignment of building a permanent temple. "When Solomon had finished building the temple of the Lord . . . the Lord said to him: 'I have heard the prayer and plea you have made before me; I have consecrated this temple, which you have built, by putting my Name there forever. My eyes and my heart will always be there'" (1 Kings 9:1-3).

So it is no wonder that the psalmist envied the birds who had unrestricted access to the temple.

> *Even the sparrow has found a home,*
> *and the swallow a nest for herself,*
> *where she may have her young—*
> *a place near your altar,*
> *O Lord Almighty, my King and my God.*
> *Blessed are those who dwell in your house;*
> *they are ever praising you.*

Then the psalmist makes a shift. Those are blessed who can be "on location," but so are those who desire to be there.

> *Blessed are those whose strength is in you,*
> *who have set their hearts on pilgrimage.*

A pilgrimage is a sacred journey. The Israelites regularly made pilgrimages to Jerusalem, but the psalmist realized that God's blessing is on those who set their *hearts* on pilgrimage.

Then the psalmist bores to the heart of what it will mean to set your heart on pilgrimage. You will not calibrate with culture. The pilgrim's sacred quest will match him against culture. But the heavenly-minded pilgrim will do the earth good.

> *As they pass through the Valley of Baca,*
> *they make it a place of springs;*
> *the autumn rains also cover it with pools.*
> *They go from strength to strength,*
> *till each appears before God in Zion.*

Baca is an obscure Hebrew word. The root word means "balsam tree" or "to weep." Balsam trees are common in arid valleys.

So the psalmist is saying that pilgrims will pass through sorrowful and parched places. He does not say *if* they pass through these places; this is an accepted fact. The point is that when a pilgrim passes through the dry places and the places of weeping in life, she will make them places of springs.

She will make it . . . this is a choice she can and will make. Because she has been redeemed, she is free from bondage to a self-centered perspective of her place of weeping. Because she has a pilgrim perspective, she sees the dry places redemptively, and she reacts to them redemptively. But then notice what happens.

"The autumn rains also cover it with pools." When she makes this pilgrim choice and turns her dry place into an oasis, then God's grace rushes in, and her spring of obedience becomes pools of blessing for other weary travelers. And she goes from strength to strength, giving a clearer and brighter reflection of her redemption.

Each dry place has the potential to make the pilgrim even stronger until at last her quest is over and she reaches the celestial city.

Ruth had a pilgrim perspective.

A PILGRIM'S PURSUIT

Ruth Yarbrough became a Christian in 1954. She was twenty-nine years old. "Soon after I became a Christian," Ruth told me, "I read Paul's words in Philippians 3:10: 'I want to know Christ and the power of his resurrection and the fellowship of sharing in his sufferings, becoming like him in his death.'"

Ruth continued, "This became my prayer. I longed to know Christ better, and soon He showed me Galatians 2:20: 'I have been crucified with Christ and I no longer live, but Christ lives in me. The life I live in the body, I live by faith in the Son of God, who loved me and gave himself for me.'"

Then Ruth shared other Scriptures that had guided her in her Christian life.

"Give thanks in all circumstances, for this is God's will for you in Christ Jesus" (1 Thessalonians 5:18).

"Do not conform any longer to the pattern of this world, but be transformed by the renewing of your mind. Then you will be able to test and approve what God's will is—his good, pleasing and perfect will" (Romans 12:2).

"And we know that in all things God works for the good of those who love him, who have been called according to his purpose. For those God foreknew he also predestined to be conformed to the likeness of his Son, that he might be the firstborn among many brothers" (Romans 8:28-29).

And she said that Philippians 1:6 was a great comfort: "Being confident of this, that he who began a good work in you will carry it on to completion until the day of Christ Jesus."

Ruth shared all of this just after she was diagnosed with Parkinson's disease. "I was not programmed to be inactive, so this is not easy. I do not enjoy my condition, but God's Word holds me together in His hand. Now I know as a fact the truth of 2 Corinthians 12:9: 'My grace is sufficient for you, for my power is made perfect in weakness.'" Then she added, with her characteristic twinkle in her eyes, "I suspect I will know this even more in the months to come."

Over the next months as Ruth gradually had to use a cane, then a walker, then a wheelchair, and finally was confined to bed, I would frequently ask her, "Do you know Him better? Is it enough? Is His grace sufficient?" The answer was always the same, a triumphant yes! Even when she could no longer speak and was so weak and frail that she could barely move, I would lean over and ask her my questions, and she would nod her head. The sparkle was still in her eyes.

This pilgrim's pursuit to know Christ better has now ended. She sees Him face to face and knows Him in all His glory.

A PILGRIM'S PROGRESS

John Bunyan's allegory *Pilgrim's Progress* portrays the life of Christian as he journeys from the City of Destruction to the

Celestial City. One thing Christian learns along the way is that there are no shortcuts. When he detours from the narrow path, he finds himself in Doubting Castle being terrorized by Giant Despair. A detour may look like a quicker and easier route, but in reality our progress will be obstructed.

Sanctification is that work of God's Spirit whereby we die to sin and live to righteousness. When the disciples of John the Baptist became concerned that everyone was going to Jesus to be baptized, John did not succumb to self-promotion or self-protection. He cut to the chase: "He must become greater; I must become less" (John 3:30).

Jesus occupying more space in my life and me taking up less space means dying to self and living to righteousness: repentance and faith. There is no way around it. And dying to self is the hard part. We cannot die to what we have not recognized, and our hearts are "deceitful above all things" (Jeremiah 17:9).

The Puritans realized this and prayed for the "gift of tears" over their sin.

Elizabeth Prentiss knew this and wrote: "I will not tolerate anything wrong in myself. I hate, I hate sin against my God and Saviour, and sin against the earthly friends whom I love with such a passionate intensity that they are able to wring my heart out, and always will be, if I live to be a hundred."[3]

The Westminster Assembly knew this. To the question "What is repentance unto life?" they responded: "Repentance unto life is a saving grace, whereby a sinner, out of a true sense of his sin, and apprehension of the mercy of God in Christ, doth, with grief and hatred of his sin, turn from it unto God, with full purpose of, and endeavor after, new obedience."[4]

There is no instant sanctification. There is no easy formula. We must exercise our spiritual muscles and take hold of the promises of God. We must go through the basic spiritual disciplines of Bible study, prayer, fasting, worship, and fellowship.

This is progress. This is the path of obedience.

A PILGRIM'S PATH

The pilgrim path is the path of blessing. Note again what the psalmist said:

> Blessed are those whose strength is in you,
> who have set their hearts on pilgrimage.

The psalmist concludes his psalm with another triumphant affirmation of the pilgrim's blessing: "O Lord Almighty, blessed is the man who trusts in you."

The psalmist has just talked about dry and sorrowful places. How can he trivialize that by talking about blessings? This juxtaposition is legitimate because he knew the biblical concept of blessing. Our spiritual eyesight is often distorted by the "health and wealth" gospel. We say with our mouths that we reject the "name it and claim it" theology, but like the women whose conversations are recorded in chapter 2, we fall into this trap when the path becomes rough. "Why isn't God blessing me? Why am I having such a difficult time? Why isn't my life more pleasant?"

We need a biblical understanding of blessing.

There are two verbs in Hebrew that mean to bless. One is *barak* and the other is *'ashar*. Understanding both words is essential to comprehending this concept.

The *Theological Wordbook of the Old Testament* says that:

> ... when *barak* is used the initiative comes from God. God can bestow his blessing even when man doesn't deserve it. On the other hand, to be blessed (*'ashar*), man has to do something. ... Usually this is something positive. A "blessed" man, for example, is one who trusts in God without equivocation ... who comes under the authority of God's revelation. ... The man who is beneficent to the poor is blessed. ...[5]

'Ashar is the word used in Psalm 84. So walking the pilgrim path is to walk in the way of obedience. The *New Geneva Study*

Bible's comment on this word is that blessed is "a stronger word than 'happy'; to be 'blessed' is to enjoy God's special favor and grace."

The other word used throughout the Old Testament (*barak*) is probably nowhere more clearly seen than in the Aaronic benediction in Numbers 6:24-26:

> *The Lord bless you and keep you;*
> *the Lord make his face shine upon you*
> *and be gracious to you;*
> *the Lord turn his face toward you*
> *and give you peace.*

In commenting on *barak*, the *Theological Wordbook* says:

> . . . the OT sees God as the only source. As such he controls blessing and cursing (Numbers 22f.). His presence confers blessing (2 Samuel 6:11-20), and it is only in his name that others can confer blessing (Deuteronomy 10:8, etc.). Indeed, God's name, the manifestation of his personal, redemptive, covenant-keeping nature, is at the heart of all blessing. As a result, those who are wrongly related to God can neither bless (Malachi 2:2) nor be blessed (Deuteronomy 28), and no efficacious word can alter this. . . .[6]

The *New Geneva Study Bible* says, "The pronouncement of this blessing placed God's covenant name LORD (Yahweh) on the people."

Blessing and cursing are used interchangeably with life and death. The heart of the Old Testament concept is that blessing is linked to reproductive powers, which belong only to God who is the life-giver. This reaches its ultimate expression in John 3:16: "For God so loved the world that he gave his one and only Son, that whoever believes in him shall not perish but have eternal life."

To reduce blessing to external, temporal gain is to misunderstand and minimize the eternal plan and purpose of God for His people. Blessing (*barak*) involves redemption from the curse of death to an eternal, covenant relationship with the living God. Blessing (*'ashar*) involves our unwavering trust in and response to this truth. The two together provide a kingdom mentality, a transcendent reality that brings magnificence to the seemingly mundane, and glory to the seemingly gory.

Elizabeth Prentiss understood this. Though she suffered poor health, chronic insomnia, and the death of a child, her husband wrote:

> Her faith never failed; she glorified God in the midst of it all; she thanked her Lord and Master for "taking her in hand," and begged Him not to spare her for her crying, if so be she might thus learn to love Him more and grow more like Him! And, what is especially noteworthy, her own suffering, instead of paralyzing, as severe suffering sometimes does, active sympathy with the sorrows and trials of others, had just the contrary effect. "How soon," she wrote to a friend, "our dear Lord presses our experiences into His own service! How many lessons He teaches us in order to make us sons (or daughters) of consolation!"[7]

Her letter to a friend crosses all time boundaries. It is as applicable to the woman who is suffering today as it was in 1871.

> If I need make any apology for writing you so often, it must be this—I can not help it. Having dwelt long in an obscure, oftentimes dark valley, and then passed out into a bright plane of life, I am full of tender yearnings over other souls, and would gladly spend my whole time and strength for them. I long, especially, to see your feet established on an immovable Rock. It seems to me that God is preparing you for great usefulness by the fiery trial of your faith. "They learn in suffering what they teach in song." Oh how true this

is! Who is so fitted to sing praises to Christ as he who has learned Him in hours of bereavement, disappointment and despair?

. . . Faith is His, unbelief ours. No process of reasoning can soothe a mother's empty, aching heart, or bring Christ into it to fill up all that great waste room. But faith can. And faith is His gift; a gift to be won by prayer—prayer persistent, patient, determined; prayer that will take no denial; prayer that if it goes away one day unsatisfied, keeps on saying, "Well, there's to-morrow and to-morrow and to-morrow; God may wait to be gracious, and I can wait to receive, but receive I must and will." . . . This is all heart, not head work. Do I know what I am talking about? Yes, I do. But my intellect is of no use to me when my heart is breaking. I must get down on my knees and own that I am less than nothing, seek God, not joy; consent to suffer, not cry for relief. And how transcendently good He is when He brings me down to that low place and there shows me that that self-renouncing, self-despairing spot is just the one where He will stoop to meet me!

My dear friend, don't let this great tragedy of sorrow fail to do everything for you. It is a dreadful thing to lose children; but a lost sorrow is the most fearful experience life can bring. I feel this so strongly that I could go on writing all day. It has been said that the intent of sorrow is to "toss us on to God's promises." Alas, these waves too often toss us away out to sea, where neither sun or stars appear for many days. I pray, earnestly, that it may not be so with you.[8]

A PILGRIM PRINCIPLE

There is a basic biblical principle that the women in the conversations mentioned in chapter 2 had missed. In almost every conversation, someone was indebted to the woman. A husband had deserted, a child had disappointed, a circumstance had deprived. But the redemptive principle is a principle of release from debt. Old Testament law commanded:

> *If a fellow Hebrew, a man or a woman, sells himself to you and serves you six years, in the seventh year you must let him go free. And when you release him, do not send him away empty-handed. Supply him liberally from your flock, your threshing floor and your winepress. Give to him as the Lord your God has blessed you. Remember that you were slaves in Egypt and the Lord your God redeemed you. That is why I give you this command today.*
>
> — *Deuteronomy 15:12-15*

Not only is the principle one of release, but one of giving. The Israelite was to release the one indebted and was actually to supply him liberally with his own goods in proportion to his blessing (*barak*) from God. What is incredible about this is that it had nothing to do with the character or performance of the indebted one; it had to do with the reality of redemption. Release of one indebted to us is a reflection of our redemption.

How do we do this?

> *Be kind and compassionate to one another, forgiving each other, just as in Christ God forgave you.*
>
> — *Ephesians 4:32*

> *Therefore, as the elect of God, holy and beloved, put on tender mercies, kindness, humbleness of mind, meekness, longsuffering; bearing with one another, and forgiving one another, if anyone has a complaint against another; even as Christ forgave you, so you also must do. But above all these things put on love, which is the bond of perfection.*
>
> — *Colossians 3:12-14 (NKJV)*

We can do this! We have been redeemed, and we are actually the dwelling place of God:

> *Don't you know that you yourselves are God's temple and that God's Spirit lives in you? If anyone destroys God's temple, God will destroy him; for God's temple is sacred, and you are that temple.*
>
> — *1 Corinthians 3:16-17*

> *Do you not know that your body is a temple of the Holy Spirit, who is in you, whom you have received from God? You are not your own; you were bought at a price. Therefore honor God with your body.*
>
> — *1 Corinthians 6:19-20*

Sometimes I long to be inside the skin of my husband and children. I want to know what makes them tick. I want to escape my limitations and know their every dream, their every hurt, their every thought. This is how God feels about us, and He is not limited. He is inside our skin, and He knows us better than we know ourselves. And even though He knows us so intimately, remember His word about His temple: "My eyes and my heart will always be there" (1 Kings 9:3).

What blessed intimacy with our Redeemer.

Oswald Chambers said:

> When once we get intimate with Jesus, we are never lonely, we never need sympathy, we can pour out all the time without being pathetic. The saint who is intimate with Jesus will never leave impressions of himself, but only the impression that Jesus is having unhindered sway, because the last abyss of his nature has been satisfied by Jesus. The only impression left by such a life is that of the strong calm sanity that our Lord gives to those who are intimate with Him.[9]

May we pray for such intimacy.

IN SUMMARY

As recipients of redemption, we are empowered to reflect our Redeemer. We live in His presence. It is our privilege and responsibility to reflect Him in all of life. True women will be "the brightest patterns of kindness and mercy which our selfish world contains," and the reflection will be so brilliant that it "cannot be unnoticed or unacknowledged. . . . " It will be especially lustrous when she releases one who is indebted to her by forgiving that individual even as God has forgiven her.

Personal Reflection

1. Read Psalm 84. Are you in a valley of weeping? Have you made it a place of springs by reflecting the reality of your redemption in that dry place? Ask God for grace to turn your dry place into an oasis.

2. Reread the verses that guided Ruth Yarbrough in her pursuit of knowing and becoming like Christ. Make your own list of such verses. Write them in your journal so you can return to them when you need to refocus.

3. Read Deuteronomy 15:12-15. Is there anyone who is indebted to you whom you have not released by forgiveness? It does not matter whether the person has asked for forgiveness. Your responsibility is to forgive, because you had a debt and God forgave you.

4. Read 1 Kings 9:1-3 and write a prayer in your journal rejoicing that God's eyes and His heart are always with you.

$\mathcal{F}$INANCIAL CRISIS

Comprehending the love of our sovereign God has always baffled me, especially since the love I have for others is often conditional and His is just the opposite. Oswald Chambers, writing about redemptive reality, said, "The worst and vilest can never get to the bottom of His love." God's great love for me and my family was magnified when we came to the end of our ropes financially.

My husband and I were hard workers and equally good at spending the money we made. I suppose like many we were caught up in the easy-credit cycle and were living beyond our means. Our bills were paid ahead of time, but living from week to week left us no reserves or savings. Everything fell apart when my husband lost his good-paying job. For the next six months we were without work and cash. For us then it was the worst of times. Now looking back, I can thankfully say it was really the best of times too. At the time, however, I felt totally humiliated, frightened, and ashamed and knew that we had only one place left to turn to, and that was to Jesus for help. Part of me cried out to God, "What did I do to deserve this harsh spanking?" But God showed us His mercy, grace, and compassion by lovingly providing for us through His covenant family. He was our Jehovah Jireh (our provider).

Our local church family was marvelous in their tenderness as they cared for us. We felt no judgment as naughty children but only loving forgiveness. They faithfully provided for us week after week by praying and through provisions of groceries, meals, and money to pay the bills. Many families had us over for delicious meals and times of wonderful fellowship. Almost every week we received encouraging notes that pointed us to Christ and said that they were praying for us to find work and for Jesus to protect our family. When we had to return a leased car to the dealer, the very next day one of our church members sold us a car for one dollar!

Three special women from our church were wonderful soul mates. Pat, Debbie, and Maggie encouraged and prayed with me and assured me that the circumstances we were experiencing were part of God's sovereign plan for our lives and that something good would come from them. They cried and laughed with me, and through it all they stuck like glue.

I vividly remember the day we had to tell our daughter that we were destitute. After hearing the news and then crying together, she said, "Mom and Daddy, we'll just have to lean on Jesus." But I was so fearful for our daughter because she was attending a Christian high school, and with no money available for tuition she would have to change midterm to the local public high school. God graciously intervened, and she was given a full scholarship. This one special answer to our prayers renewed my trust and faith.

Weeks turned into months, and although my husband worked diligently trying to find a job, work just didn't come. My anchor Scripture that kept my eyes on Jesus and His redemptive love for us was Isaiah 43:1-3 (NKJV): "Fear not, for I have redeemed you; I have called you by your name; you are mine. When you pass through the waters, I will be with you; and through the rivers, they shall not overflow you. When you walk through the fire, you shall not be burned. Nor shall the flame scorch you. For I am the Lord your God, the Holy One of Israel, your Savior."

Finally God wonderfully answered our prayers and gave my husband a position out of state. That was not our plan for sure, as we wanted so much to stay in Illinois with our friends and church family. We were forced to leave our loving, supportive church family and relocate in Oklahoma City.

Out of this difficult experience, Jesus brought us to the lowest point in our lives to show us that we can only depend upon Him. Now we strive to live for Christ and His church out of thanksgiving and not because of obligation. It is all of grace; no part of it is mine.

— Carolyn Muse
Oklahoma City

$\mathscr{A}$ CULTIVATOR
OF COMMUNITY

Let the general tone of female morals be low, and all will be rendered nugatory: while the universal prevalence of womanly intelligence and virtue will swell the stream of civilization to its highest level, impregnate it with its richest qualities, and spread its fertility over the widest surface. A community is not likely to be overthrown where woman fulfills her mission; for by the power of her noble heart over the hearts of others, she will raise it from its ruins, and restore it again to prosperity and joy.

Female Piety

The new woman is stridently challenged to individualism and self-fulfillment, but the true woman is uniquely equipped and commissioned to be a cultivator of community.

We hear a lot about community today. It sometimes refers to people living in the same locality and under the same government (the Atlanta community), a social group with a common interest (the arts community), and groups with a common identity (the business community). There is commonality of location or interest, but the individual maintains autonomy in determining when he or she will join a community and when to leave. It is distressing that many Christians approach church membership with this understanding of community.

This superficial understanding of community pales in comparison to the biblical concept. The popular conception of community is another counterfeit.

The true woman belongs to a true community.

TRUE COMMUNITY

The biblical meaning of community flows from the covenant. Covenant encapsulates all that is involved in our relationship with God, and it also gives definition to our relationships with one another.

Whereas salvation is a very individual and personal matter, we do not live in isolation. In Genesis 17:5, God revealed the covenant to Abraham and promised that Abraham would be

> *a father of many nations. I will make you very fruitful; I will make nations of you, and kings will come from you. I will establish my covenant as an everlasting covenant between me and you and your descendants after you for the generations to come, to be your God and the God of your descendants after you. The whole land of Canaan, where you are now an alien, I will give as an everlasting possession to you and your descendants after you; and I will be their God.*
>
> *— Genesis 17:5-8*

After the death, resurrection, and ascension of Jesus, God reiterated this promise when Peter said in his Pentecost sermon, "Repent and be baptized, every one of you, in the name of Jesus Christ for the forgiveness of your sins. And you will receive the gift of the Holy Spirit. The promise is for you and your children and for all who are far off—for all whom the Lord our God will call" (Acts 2:38-39).

The people in Malachi's day were discouraged. They doubted God's covenant promises and His covenant love. It started with the priests, so God rebuked them: "'For the lips of a priest ought to preserve knowledge, and from his mouth men should seek instruction—because he is the messenger of the Lord Almighty. But you have turned from the way and by your teaching have caused many to stumble; you have violated the covenant with Levi,' says the Lord Almighty" (Malachi 2:7-8).

A lack of knowledge of God's covenant love led to a break-down in their covenant relationships with one another. "Have we not all one Father? Did not one God create us? Why do we profane the covenant of our fathers by breaking faith with one another?" (Malachi 2:10).

Malachi goes on to tell the people that the Lord does not accept their offerings because He "is acting as the witness between you and the wife of your youth, because you have broken faith with her, though she is your partner, the wife of your marriage covenant" (Malachi 2:14).

Doubting God's covenant love moved from the unfaithful religious leaders to community relationships and to family relationships. The results were widespread. They always are. God said that the people had robbed Him. When they asked how they had robbed Him, He replied: "In tithes and offerings. You are under a curse—the whole nation of you—because you are robbing me. Bring the whole tithe into the storehouse, that there may be food in my house" (Malachi 3:8-10a).

The storehouse was a room in the temple designated for storing gifts. Failure to take the tithe to the storehouse was a community matter, and it brought a curse on the whole community.

But God continued to hold out the promise and to remind the people that obedience would bring blessing to the community. "'Test me in this,' says the Lord Almighty, 'and see if I will not throw open the floodgates of heaven and pour out so much blessing that you will not have room enough for it. I will prevent pests from devouring your crops, and the vines in your fields will not cast their fruit,' says the Lord Almighty. 'Then all the nations will call you blessed, for yours will be a delightful land,' says the Lord Almighty" (Malachi 3:10b-12).

Some continued to be faithless and arrogant, but some coalesced again into a community of faith: "Then those who feared the Lord talked with each other, and the Lord listened and heard. A scroll of remembrance was written in his presence concerning those who feared the Lord and honored his name. 'They will be mine,' says the Lord Almighty, 'in the day when I make up my treasured possession. I will spare them, just as in compassion a man spares his son who serves him'" (3:16-17).

God is jealously possessive of His treasured possession. A breakdown in His covenant community is no trivial matter. The source and sustenance of our solidarity as a community is our covenant relationship with God. Paul drives this point home in his letter to the Ephesians.

After meticulously outlining the redemptive work of the Father, Son, and Holy Spirit in purposing, accomplishing, and applying our salvation, Paul reminds us that it was grace that translated us from objects of wrath to objects of mercy. He emphasizes our former condition: "remember that at that time you were separate from Christ, excluded from citizenship in Israel and foreigners to the covenants of the promise, without hope and without God in the world" (Ephesians 2:12).

Separate, excluded, foreigners, without hope—these words describe how many people today feel. It is said that the greatest cause of stress today is isolation. People feel disconnected and alone. One young woman told me that she had always felt rejection. "But then God saved me, and now I know what it means to belong. I belong to Him and to His people."

Paul continues, "But now in Christ Jesus you who once were far away have been brought near through the blood of Christ" (Ephesians 2:13).

Then he transitions to the resulting existence of the covenant community: "Consequently, you are no longer foreigners and aliens, but fellow citizens with God's people and members of God's household, built on the foundation of the apostles and prophets, with Christ Jesus himself as the chief cornerstone. In him the whole building is joined together and rises to become a holy temple in the Lord. And in him you too are being built together to become a dwelling in which God lives by his Spirit" (Ephesians 2:19-22).

The stuff of which this community is held together is not self-determined commonality; it is grace. The foundation is not common locality or interest; it is Christ Jesus. Our covenant connection with Him binds us together in covenant with one another. This is the essence and vitality of the church, God's covenant community.

COMMUNITY PRIVILEGES
AND RESPONSIBILITIES

The Puritans understood the privileges and the responsibilities of the covenant community. The Westminster Assembly wrote: "All saints, that are united to Jesus Christ, their Head, by His Spirit, and by faith, have fellowship with Him in His grace, sufferings, death, resurrection, and glory: and, being united to one another in love, they have communion in each other's gifts and graces, and are obliged to the performance of such duties, public and private, as do conduce to their mutual good, both in the inward and outward man."[1]

Think of that! I am obliged to share my gifts and graces with you and to perform whatever duties promote the mutual good of the church. This explains why Mary Fish and Elizabeth Prentiss put such a high premium on duty. This also eliminates a consumer, felt-needs approach to church membership. The question is not "what am I getting out of this?" but "how am I to touch the lives of others in my church with grace and mercy?"

The Westminster Confession continues: "Saints by profession are bound to maintain an holy fellowship and communion in the worship of God, and in performing such other spiritual services as tend to their mutual edification; as also in relieving each other in outward things, according to their several abilities and necessities. Which communion, as God offereth opportunity, is to be extended unto all those who, in every place, call upon the name of the Lord Jesus."[2]

It was this understanding of community that the Puritans who settled America brought with them. It was this understanding of covenant that formed the soul of America. John Winthrop, first governor of Massachusetts Bay Colony, wrote:

This love among Christians is a real thing, not imaginary
. . . as absolutely necessary to the (well) being of the Body of
Christ, as the sinews and other ligaments of a natural body are
to the (well) being of that body. . . . We are a company, pro-
fessing ourselves fellow members of Christ, (and thus) we
ought to account ourselves knit together by this bond of love.
. . . Thus stands the cause between God and us: we are entered
into covenant with Him for this work. . . . For this end, we
must be knit together in this work as one man. . . . We must
delight in each other, make one another's condition our own,
rejoice together, mourn together, labor and suffer together,
always having before our eyes our Commission and
Community in this work, as members of the same body. So
shall we keep the unity of the Spirit in the bond of peace. . . .

We shall find that the God of Israel is among us, when ten
of us shall be able to resist a thousand of our enemies, when
He shall make us a praise and glory, that men of succeeding
plantations shall say, 'The Lord make it like that of New
England.' For we must consider that we shall be as a City
upon a Hill. . . .[3]

This flies in the face of another of our cultural idols—individualism. But it's not just culture that steers us toward independence.
Our sinful bent to self-rule and self-containment was heard early
on in human history. When Cain's jealousy erupted and he killed
his brother Abel, God asked, "Where is your brother?" Cain's reply,
"Am I my brother's keeper?" has reverberated down through the
ages. The cry of the unregenerate is "I am not responsible for you."
No earthly "community" can override this proclivity. But the community of grace can truly be knit together in love. Our covenant
relationship with the Lord God empowers us to be covenant-keep-
ers. I am my brothers' and sisters' keeper.

Everything I have said applies equally to men and women. In
Christ there is "neither Jew nor Greek, slave nor free, male nor
female, for you are all one in Christ Jesus" (Galatians 3:28).

When we gather around the Lord's table for the Lord's Supper to commemorate His death till He comes again and to celebrate our membership in the church and our community with Christ and with each other, there is no distinction. But when we leave the table with a renewed zeal for service, our gender does sometimes take us in different directions. In some kingdom work we stand side by side with men, but at other times there are things that men do better and other things that women do better. God designed it that way.

WOMAN BY DESIGN

I will not belabor this point since I have discussed it at length in my book *By Design*. But before we consider how the true woman is a cultivator of true community, I will give a brief overview of our creational design.

In Genesis 2:18 the Lord God said, "It is not good for the man to be alone. I will make a helper suitable for him."

Being appointed as a helper is not a second-class assignment. Throughout the Old Testament God often describes Himself as our Helper.

The Hebrew word for helper is *ezer*. In commenting on this word, the *Theological Wordbook of the Old Testament* explains, "The Lord is seen as the helper of the underprivileged: the poor (Psalm 72:12) and the fatherless (Psalm 10:14). . . . The psalmist is conscious of divine assistance at a time of illness (Psalm 28:7), at a time of oppression by enemies (Psalm 54:4), and at a time of great personal distress (Psalm 86:17)."[4]

This explanation of how God is our *ezer* gives us insight into the helper role. The ways that God is our Helper can be summarized into two categories: community and compassion. God enters into a loving, protecting relationship with His people (community). He comes to our aid, comforts us, and is merciful toward us (compassion).

This touches our feminine souls because entering into nurturing relationships and extending compassion to those in need is part of our helper design. Our design equips us to infuse community and compassion into our relationships. Women will do this in various ways. We are not clones. Our strengths, temperaments, experiences, opportunities, life stage, and interests will be factors in how we fulfill this design. This concept has application to us as individuals, and it also gives definition to our corporate mission.

Our corporate ministry as women in God's church should have the effect of bringing a deeper sense of community and compassion into our church family. We will discuss compassion in the next chapter, but now let us proceed with our discussion of how women can cultivate community.

You may be thinking that this will begin with a discussion of fellowship dinners and nursery duty. I am in no way minimizing these ministries, but this is not the starting point for cultivating community. I think we get some clues from Deborah the prophetess.

VILLAGE LIFE

The book of Judges recounts the repeated cycle of the Israelites' disobedience to the covenant, God handing them over to their enemies, their cry for help, and God providing a judge to deliver them. The repeated phrase "everyone did what was right in his own eyes" indicates their violation of their covenant relationship with God and with one another.

"After Ehud died, the Israelites once again did evil in the eyes of the Lord. So the Lord sold them into the hands of Jabin, a king of Canaan . . . " (Judges 4:1-2).

When the Israelites cried out to the Lord, He raised up Deborah. Following the defeat of Jabin, Deborah sang a song of praise (5:2-31):

> " . . . *the roads were abandoned;*
> *travelers took to winding paths.*
> *Village life in Israel ceased,*

> *ceased until I, Deborah arose,*
> *arose a mother in Israel.*
> *When they chose new gods,*
> *war came to the city gates,*
> *and not a shield or spear was seen*
> *among forty thousand in Israel."*

Roads were abandoned because they were not safe. Isolation, idolatry, suffering, and fear prevailed. There was no village life, no community among God's covenant people, until God raised up a mother in Israel.

It would be easy to romanticize this and to conjure up sentimental images of this mother in Israel. But the truth is, Deborah was a tiger! When Barak, fully aware of the odds in a battle against Jabin's commander Sisera and his nine hundred chariots of iron, refused to lead the Israelites into battle unless Deborah went along, she did not waver. Not only did Deborah lead her people into a bloody battle, but another woman, Jael, drove a tent peg through Sisera's skull. These women meant business.

In one of the *ezer* verses, David wrote: "Strangers are attacking me; ruthless men seek my life—men without regard for God. Selah. Surely God is my help (*ezer*); the Lord is the one who sustains me" (Psalm 54:3-4). God is our Helper when we are oppressed by enemies. He is our Protector and Defender.

When the covenant community was threatened, Deborah and Jael leaped into action.

It is not always enemies in chariots that threaten community life. Sometimes it is theological enemies that seek to undercut the foundations of the community. This was the threat to Jenny Geddes's community.

SCOTLAND'S NATIONAL COVENANT

On a tour tracing our Presbyterian heritage, we traipsed through many wonderful sites in England and Scotland. One of the highlights for Gene and me was St. Giles Cathedral in Edinburgh. I took a picture of Gene standing beside a life-size statue of his hero John Knox. He took a picture of me standing beside a monument of a three-legged stool on a pedestal, because it was there that I found a new heroine.

Jenny Geddes was an ordinary fruit seller, but on July 23, 1637, she followed in the footsteps of Deborah and Jael. The foundation of the covenant community was in danger, and she refused to sit on her stool and watch.

When Charles I became king, he demanded that religious practices in Scotland conform to the English model. He was an Anglican, and he tried to impose that liturgy on the Scottish church. The prayer book was read for the first time in St. Giles on July 23. In those days, there were no pews. The congregation stood or brought their own stools. Apparently Jenny had a stool.

When the bishop began reading from the prayer book, the congregation was paralyzed in a stunned silence until Jenny yelled, "Thou false priest! Wouldst thou say mass at my lug (ear)," picked up her stool, and threw it toward the pulpit. With that a riot broke out, and throughout the church stools became missiles. This riot led eventually to the signing of the National Covenant that rejected the divine right of kings in favor of man's duty to God. The National Covenant formed the core of Scotland's national character.

Let me hasten to clarify. I am not suggesting that women drive pegs through the skulls of their enemies or throw stools at their preachers, even if they are preaching false or watered-down doctrine. What I am saying is that cultivating community is much more than having fellowship dinners.

It means having such a profound commitment to the biblical concept of community that we will not stand by when the basic principles of that community are being attacked.

It means being intentional as we go about the ministries of planning fellowship dinners, visiting the bereaved, and taking food to the sick. It means understanding that these ministries are sacred because they are kingdom activities. A secular service organization may do many of the same things we do, but our motive must be different, or we will soon drift into being little more than another secular service organization. Our motive must be to create and cultivate a sense of family among God's people, or these ministries will become form without substance.

Something that must be said, though it may be difficult for some to hear, is that the woman who is married will not infuse real community into any relationship if she is not doing it in her marriage. This does not mean that the marriage will necessarily be a loving one. The woman cannot determine her husband's response. Neither does it mean that the marriage will endure. Again the woman cannot control her husband's actions. But it does mean that even if the husband defaults, the wife's attitude is one of love, acceptance, and forgiveness because she is doing all she can to protect the marriage covenant. She reflects her redemption in releasing (forgiving) one indebted to her.

Women who follow in the tradition of Deborah, Jael, and Jenny Geddes are often found on their knees in prayer defending their families and the church of Jesus Christ against the evil one.

COVENANT-KEEPERS

In *The Micah Mandate*, George Grant issues a clarion call to Christians to return to this understanding of the church:

> ... culture is the temporal manifestation of a people's faith. If a culture begins to change, it is not because of fads, fashions, or the passing of time; it is because of a shift in worldview— it is because of a change of faith. Thus, race, ethnicity, folklore, politics, language, or heritage are simply expressions of a deeper paradigm rooted in the covenantal and spiritual matrix of a community's church and the integrity of its witness. . . . the future of our culture depends upon ordinary men and women in the church who are willing to live lives of justice, mercy, and humility before God. . . .

Writing to one of her many literary friends, the remarkable blind-deaf-mute, Helen Keller said: "I long to accomplish a great and noble task, but it is my chief duty to accomplish humble tasks as though they were great and noble. The world is moved along not by the mighty shoves of its heroes, but by the aggregate of the tiny pushes of each honest worker. . . ."

Now it is time for all of us who comprise the aggregate to begin to live out the prophetic implications of that kind of faith ourselves by accomplishing the humble tasks of the church's ministry to the world—as though they were great and noble. It is time for us to change the world with our tiny pushes of justice, mercy, and humble faith.[5]

COVENANT CAMEOS

The tiny pushes of women I have observed are a delicate engraving on our cultural landscape. . . .

The widow I met who told me about the leadership crisis in her church and the declining membership, but whose face brightened as she told me that for ten years she and a friend had met together every week to pray for their church.

Women who lovingly and joyfully plan family reunions and celebrations in order to create family memories and traditions.

Women who implement Titus 2 programs in their church so that women are connected in covenant relationships.

The women in the church in Decatur, Alabama, who reached out to our daughter Kathryn even before she and Dean moved to their community. They knew she was coming, and they must have known what it would be like for her to leave her "root system" and relocate. She received a card from the women's Bible study telling her they were praying for her. Then a woman called and said they would bring meals for a week when she moved in. Though the idea of moving with four children was scary, Kathryn said, "I haven't met them, but I already feel attached."

Women like Paige Winck, an attorney in Knoxville, Tennessee, who intentionally strives to integrate her faith into her professional life. Paige coordinates a lunch hour study group for working women in her community and, with accountant Renda Burkhart, leads outreach groups for women executives. By discussing from a biblical perspective such issues as the source of a woman's personal identity, the nature of women's work, and the spiritual disciplines, these employed women are strengthening one another in their faith.

The women who take the ministry of hospitality seriously. They welcome people into their homes in obedience to God's Word to "entertain strangers, for by so doing some people have entertained angels without knowing it" (Hebrews 13:2).

The women in my church who faithfully attend wedding and baby showers, even when they do not know the young honoree. "They are part of our church family, and this is one way we will get to know them," I often hear them say.

My friend Sarah quietly moving to sit beside a young woman who was going through a divorce and who was sitting alone at church. The young woman told me later, "I felt so alone. Then Sarah slipped beside me, put her arm around me, and gave me a hug. I felt loved."

Audrey Stallings, a retiree who is so compelled by the Titus 2 principle of women nurturing women that she took it with her to Russia on a short-term missions trip. "I prayed that somehow I would be able to cross the language and cultural barriers and reach the Russian women with the truth of the Titus principle. When I spoke to them in a church gathering, I explained that I was going to pair the older and younger women for prayer. They literally did not know how to do this. I actually had to take the hand of a younger woman and walk her to an older woman. I told them to share prayer requests with each other. What took place before my very eyes was remarkable. Once the women began talking, their cold, stoic, fearful expressions changed to freedom, release, and joy. I have never witnessed such a radical transformation. We participated in four other services in the following days, and the transformation in the relationships of the women was progressive."

The women who use their creative abilities to add warmth to the appearance and functions of their church. Flowers, beautifully served refreshments, and a friendly smile can make a church feel like home.

Women who intentionally reach beyond their ethnic environment to build real friendships with sisters of other races.

As John Winthrop said, "This love among Christians is a real thing, not imaginary. . . . " And it is this kind of love that will mark us as the covenant community and that will validate to the world that the Father sent Jesus and that He loves us even as He loves Jesus (John 17:23).

Women really do have an instinctive capacity to form relationships and to cultivate a sense of family. Elizabeth Prentiss said it well: "What a queer way we womenkind have of confiding in each other with perfectly reckless disregard of consequences! It is a mercy that men are, for the most part, more prudent, though not half so delightful!"[6]

A COVENANT CELEBRATION

The stories of two women celebrate the reality of the covenant community. The dissimilarity of these stories encourage and inspire because the difference dissolves at the Cross. The stories intersect at the point of grace. Both stories are best told in the women's own words.

Mary Matthews Burton

"This is the story of my covenant family. In 1850 Harvey Milton Mayes became a charter member of Midway Presbyterian Church in Marietta, Georgia. His son Luke married Octavia Kemp, and she gave birth to a daughter, Haddie, in 1876. Haddie was raised at Midway, married in 1911, and had a daughter Otelia Terry, my grandmother.

"About this same time, Mary Orr married Charles Pinkney

Scott, and they began attending Midway. They were friends of James and Ella Maye Echols. One couple had a son, and one had a daughter; these two children grew up and married each other. They had three sons; the oldest was Herbert Scott, my grandfather.

"Granddaddy tells me that Otelia was a tall, attractive girl with a beautiful heart for God, and it wasn't long before they fell in love. Their oldest daughter, Dianne, is my mother. Mom grew up in Midway Church, married my dad, Bob Matthews, and they had two children. My brother Charles and I were born into the Midway family and became sixth-generation members of this church. Biological and church family all merged into one happy mix. We are both, with our spouses and children, members of Midway Church.

"It was at church camp that I prayed to receive God's gift of salvation. I understood that I was a sinner and that only through Jesus Christ was it possible to have eternal life. I am so thankful for the biblical foundations that were laid throughout my life. My parents taught me the Bible. In church we memorized Scripture and The Westminster Shorter Catechism. In youth group we learned about how to grow in our relationship with the Lord.

"It was in college that I first started struggling with the issues of the sovereignty of God. Was it my choice that I became a Christian? Was it bound to happen, considering my upbringing? The more I studied, the more I embraced covenant theology.

"I learned from God's Word that before creation God chose those whom He would redeem, justify, sanctify, and glorify in Jesus Christ. The divine choice is an expression of free and sovereign grace. It is not merited by anything in those who are chosen. God owes sinners no mercy of any kind, so it is a wonder that he chose to save me!

"The Lord has richly blessed me by placing me in a family with deep roots and a godly heritage. He works beautifully through families that love Him. I know that my faith is an answer to the prayers of many saints, most of whom I never knew. My husband,

Matt, and I have a son, Luke. What a blessing to know that he, too, has generations of prayers surrounding him."

Lynn Brookside

"After surviving twenty years of spousal abuse, I left my marriage with little more than the clothes on my back and a substantial suspicion of men. A year later God led me to New Life Church in Escondido, California. When I began to learn about male headship in the church, I was tempted to 'head for the hills.' To me, men were dangerous, and any organization where men had all the authority was alarmingly dangerous.

"In addition, I was not only newly single when I came to New Life, but I was no longer occupied with the child-rearing chores that had, until recently, absorbed my time. As I watched young mothers caring for their families all around me, I felt useless and worthless. The family-oriented teachings that frequently emanated from the pulpit gave me still more reasons to feel left out and alone. I couldn't imagine why God had brought me to this place where it was so obvious I didn't fit. Once having placed me at New Life, however, God would not release me.

"It was two and a half years before I gathered the courage to be installed as a member of the church. It was the most amazing and fantastic experience! From the beginning, becoming a member of New Life had seemed to me to be a commitment parallel to a marriage commitment. I felt as if the pledge I would take—to submit to the elders—was just as serious and important as my marriage vows had been . . . with nearly the same potential for disaster. That's why I waited so long to take that step. And I took it with more than a little trepidation.

"I've tried many times to put into words the foundational change that took place in my life when I exchanged my fearful resistance to church membership for obedience. Tried and failed. Perhaps others may be able to describe it better than I, or perhaps there simply are no words in any human tongue to describe what is essentially a change in the spiritual realm.

"I can, however, express some of what has happened in my life since having been received as a member at New Life Church. As I grew to comprehend truly what it means to live covenantally, it became clear to me that I was not alone at all. In a very real way, the church is my family. The elders provide my spiritual covering, and the members are my brothers, sisters, nieces, nephews, grandchildren, and best of all, a few very special spiritual daughters. As a young wife and mother, I was busy from dawn to dusk, nurturing, encouraging, praying, and meeting the physical needs of my family. As a middle-aged single with grown children, I eventually realized that churches are composed of people who need nurturance, encouragement, prayer, and physical support.

"What's more, since becoming a member at New Life, my trust in the Lord has increased exponentially. I'm far more confident than I have ever been. Where before, fear was constant in my life, I rarely feel afraid anymore. The very thought of myself as a victim seems patently absurd. I'm a daughter of God, plain and simple! Now, rather than spending much of my emotional energy seeking places to hide and ways to avoid men, I expend my energies in ministry. My fondest desire is to bring glory to God's name.

"In short, I am a completely different person.

"Now when I hear a teaching that speaks to wives and mothers or to family life in general, I don't squirm in my seat or wish for something more pertinent to my life. I listen attentively, because I know that those teachings apply to me. I no longer watch wives and mothers nurturing their families all around me and feel useless. Instead, I recall what it was like to be a young mother and—like any good sister, aunt, or grandmother—I try to see what I can do to help. These are covenant children; their care is my responsibility also. When I see one of our young married women striving to be the kind of wife God has called her to be, I praise her for her effort and assure her that it is well worthwhile. When I see her struggling, I make time to listen to her worries and concerns and try to help dispel the fears assaulting her. And everywhere I see opportunities to encourage and equip the men and women of my church. These are not difficult things to do—they never were—but I could not see that until I got my eyes off myself and onto the Lord. I've discovered that one of my greatest needs—to glorify God and feel useful in the kingdom—is easily met . . . when I have the right perspective.

"I feel younger and more alive now than I did four years ago. And I don't feel left out, useless, worthless, or alone anymore. Every millisecond of my life is full of loving relationships and joyous activity.

"Is the correlation between these immense changes in my life and my decision to make the obedient choice—to join my church and submit to male headship—a spurious one? Would these changes have taken place in my life if I had continued to resist church membership? Possibly. I cannot prove that my assumption of a link is correct. But I believe so with all my heart. The changes in my life that followed my decision were so profound and so immediate that, as far as I'm concerned, there can be no doubt.

"I'm so very grateful that God gave me the courage not to deprive myself of the glorious joy of being a part of the body of Christ."

IN SUMMARY

God's covenant relationship with us is the source of our relationship with one another. This is the glue of the Christian community. But community life must be cultivated, and woman's helper design furnishes us with tools for the task. The true woman gives substantive, principled, diligent care to cultivating a sense of family in her home, and she collaborates and cooperates with other women to do the same in her church. This is a result of her identity as a redeemed daughter of the King.

Personal Reflection

1. Read the following passages and list in your journal the intimate, endearing terms God uses in speaking of His church:

> *John 10:16*
> *1 Corinthians 3:16; 12:27*
> *Ephesians 1:22-23; 2:19-22; 3:15; 5:23-32*
> *1 Peter 5:2-4*
> *Revelation 19:7; 21:2, 9-27.*

2. Memorize Colossians 2:2-3 and make this your prayer for your family and your church.

3. Are you cultivating community in your home? Read Proverbs 14:1 and ask God to help you to be a wise woman who builds relationships and not a foolish woman who destroys.

4. Ask God if there is someone in your family, church, or community with whom He wants you to cultivate a relationship. Invite her for tea and begin getting to know her.

5. Does your church feel like home? What are you doing to create that sense of family? Make a list of things that you and other women could do together to cultivate community in your church. Then gather with some women and pray about this.

6. Read Jesus' prayer for us in John 17:20-23. Pray this for your church.

*E*MOTIONAL STRUGGLES

At age thirty-eight, for reasons that remain a mystery, I experienced episodes of dizziness that became increasingly severe. One night I was rushed to the emergency room with an elevated heart rate and a blood pressure reading so low when I was standing that it was barely enough to sustain life. As I looked at my husband's frightened face, I held my three children in my heart, not knowing what the next few minutes would bring.

After being stabilized, I spent the next couple of days being monitored and undergoing tests without any conclusive answers. My blood pressure continued to drop whenever I stood up, but they could not pinpoint the cause. I remember my doctor's concerned face as she told me, "This is very unusual for someone your age. You've stumped us all." Inwardly, my fear, confusion, and anxiety rose. What was happening to me and why? I felt things were swirling out of control.

I was released from the hospital, but three weeks later I was so sick that I was readmitted. Through further testing a conclusion was reached as to treatment.

Even though this treatment took care of the physical problem, I struggled for months with post-traumatic stress and times of intense anxiety. I felt I had been utterly flattened and undone, and I feared a repeat of this episode in the future. The state of my health no longer seemed steady and secure.

The thread of comfort that ran throughout that time was the

love of dear friends whose tender acts of kindness, mercy, and compassion caused me to know I was not alone; I was loved. I was excited to read 2 Corinthians 7:6, "But God, who comforts the downcast, comforted us by the coming of Titus . . . " This confirmed what I was experiencing—that one means of God's comfort to us is through His body.

One friend came to the hospital even though she lived an hour's drive away. In the midst of my fear and confusion, she made me laugh, and she cried with me, too.

Another dear friend came bringing her love clothed in her trademark flowers, a tangible reminder of her love.

Another friend amazed me with her faithfulness to my needs, despite the fact that she had two small preschoolers of her own. She brought meals, drove me to doctor's appointments when I was too dizzy to drive, and even cleaned my house.

Another offered to take the kids for a night or two. Many brought meals, sent cards, prayed, called with concern, or simply embraced me at church.

Still another shared wise counsel, advising me to saturate myself in God's Word and to begin keeping a journal of the lessons God would teach me. She expressed a confidence that God would use what looked like a mess to me for His glory and purposes. I clung to that hope that she dared to have for me.

Others were willing to be vulnerable and shared similar struggles from their own past and encouraged me that there was light at the end of the tunnel.

As I struggled through the emotional aftermath, those closest to me were available with open hearts, listening ears, and encouragement. And so God's comfort flowed to me through those who sacrificed their time and convenience to be there for me.

The lessons God had and continues to have for me as I immersed myself in His Word were multifaceted. But perhaps the greatest was the fact of His sovereignty. I began to see with a new clarity that nothing we encounter on this earthly pilgrimage is by chance, meaningless, or out of His control; it is all sifted through

His hand and used by Him to accomplish His plans and purposes and to transform us into the image of His Son (Romans 8:28-29). The story of Joseph (Genesis 37-50) became a favorite. Its dramatic portrayal of this principle was a great comfort and encouragement.

God had given permission, and the hedge of protection was removed from me for a time, although I know He still enforced boundaries and limits. I walked through a valley of darkness and tasted moments of desperation that I had only heard about before. Fear was no longer a distant abstraction. It was horrifyingly real, and I felt my own weakness and vulnerability with a stark intensity. I was dependent on Him for my very breath. "For in Him we live and move and have our being" (Acts 17:28). This was now a firsthand reality.

Never would I have the courage to ask God for such an experience, but with the passage of time and a measure of healing, I am beginning to see it as a severe mercy. For out of the bitterness of this time, I began to notice a change in my heart toward the pain of others. This is not to say I have never before suffered or felt empathy toward another, but this experience brought a new depth to my capacity for compassion. No longer was I safely and comfortably removed and insulated. I began to want to wrap my heart around other individuals who were in pain, and my prayers for them took on a heartfelt cry. I now hurt with them; we have a common denominator.

By no means am I saying I have "arrived," but by all means I am saying I have grown. And the lessons continue.

In gentleness and kindness, God has opened my eyes to my own sin as a contributing factor to much of the struggle I experienced. Although I know there was a physical element, I believe there was also a sin component. I feared completely surrendering myself and my future into God's hands. I was afraid of what He might allow. I now see that the root of this was a question of authority. Did I want to be in control, or would I yield control of myself, my life, my future into the hands of our Ultimate Authority—God Himself? It seems to me this is the root of all sin.

The irony of my fear of completely surrendering myself and my future into God's hands was that I possessed neither the power nor the authority to completely control everything, and it only served to increase my distress. Francis Schaeffer has this encouraging word in his book *True Spirituality*:

> We would be less than truthful, I think, if we failed to acknowledge that often we are afraid to offer ourselves for God's use, for fear of what will come. But fear falls to the ground when we see before whom we are standing.... We are offering ourselves before the God who loves us, and He is not a monster, but our heavenly Father.... As I bow in my will in practice in this present life, it ends with communion with God as Abba, Father.

I am also learning that I need not excuse and defend my sin but that confession and repentance are a gateway to freedom from the bondage of sin. Only when I side with God in His judgment of it in my life can I begin to cooperate with His work of sanctification as I renounce it, turn from it, and engage in spiritual battle in the struggle against it. The result is increasing freedom and liberty, peace and joy.

The "theme verse" I have chosen for this year is: "Do not conform any longer to the pattern of this world, but be transformed by the renewing of your mind" (Romans 12:2).

I decided that I need to be deliberate and intentional in this business of renewing my mind. I must change my pattern of thinking. Psalm 94:19 reads: " When anxiety was great within me, your consolation brought joy to my soul." God's Word is truth (John 17:17), and the reason it has the power to bring consolation and comfort is because it is true. When anxiety is great within me (or better yet, when it is still small), I counter it with the truth of God's Word and make a new "thought pattern habit." Sometimes this means picking up pen and paper and listing reasons I have for being secure in God based on what His Word says. Then I pray that these might sink in and permeate me to the very core of my being.

Our gracious God redeems and transforms even those circumstances that are caused, or contributed to in part, by our own sin to serve His good purposes and to draw us closer to Himself. Amazing grace!

—Name withheld

ℐ CHANNEL
OF COMPASSION

*An unfeeling woman is a contradiction in terms, for the
female heart has ever been found the dwelling-place of
kindness, where misery, when all other hopes have failed,
is sure to find an asylum.*

Female Piety

Community and compassion are covenant issues. They are
marks of the family of God. For God's covenant family to
have a vital presence in culture, there must be community and
compassion in the Christian home and in the church.

A woman wrote me that she had heard me speak several times
and could never understand why I often weep as I stand before
women. "Then I was asked to be on the leadership team of the
women's ministry in our church. God gave me a vision and passion for this ministry. Now I understand your tears."

I'm not sure that I understand or can explain it, but I am driven
by it. When I stand before women, there is a surge of love and
excitement that is incredible. I see faces, but I also see families and
local churches with the potential to be safe communities from
which compassion flows. And I have the deep conviction that
women are essential for community and compassion to flourish.
Women are essential to create that family atmosphere where truth
can be heard, absorbed, and then reflected within and without the
walls of the church.

This does not constrain women. It unleashes us to do what we have been designed to do. The true woman's sanctified feminine instincts make her a channel of compassion to the afflicted and oppressed.

Again the author of *Female Piety* knew this:

> In what age, or in what country in the world, has woman forfeited her character as the ministering angel of humanity? When and where has the female bosom disowned the claims of misery and repudiated the virtue of benevolence? Arctic snows have not frozen up the springs of mercy in the female heart, nor tropical suns dried them up. Tyranny has not crushed it out, nor barbarism extinguished it. . . . Young women, cherish in your bosoms the purest philanthropy. Abhor selfishness; you are made for kindness. Oppose not the design of your Creator. Do no violence to your own nature. A stony heart becomes not you. A tearless woman is a revolting scene in our sorrowful world. She may be pure and beautiful as the marble statue, but if withal she is as hard and cold, who can admire her?[1]

COVENANT COMPASSION

The word *compassion* is from the Latin words *com*, which means with, and *pati*, which means to suffer. So it means to share a deep feeling or passion with another person. As Paul said, "Rejoice with those who rejoice; mourn with those who mourn" (Romans 12:15).

Of course, this instruction is given to all believers, but it does seem that our helper design equips us to move easily and quickly into this emotional environment. You only have to watch your little girls to know this is true. They seem to know when someone needs tender loving care, and they instinctively know how to give it. This should not surprise us. They have the helper design stamped upon them.

God reveals Himself as the helper of those needing compassion: "He will defend the afflicted among the people and save the children of the needy; he will crush the oppressor. . . . He will deliver the needy who cry out, the afflicted who have no one to help. He will take pity on the weak and the needy and save the needy from death. . . . " (Psalm 72:4, 12, 13).

So rather than recoil at the notion of being a helper, we should rejoice in this aspect of our female design. We should find great freedom in unleashing this compassionate side of our being into the arena of ministries of mercy. God created us to do this good work, and its importance to His kingdom is obvious in His instructions about making provision for the oppressed.

"When you reap the harvest of your land, do not reap to the very edges of your field or gather the gleanings of your harvest. Do not go over your vineyard a second time or pick up the grapes that have fallen. Leave them for the poor and the alien. I am the Lord your God" (Leviticus 19:9-10).

What is even more astounding is that God equates knowing Him with being compassionate to the poor and needy. In contrasting the just reign of King Josiah with the opportunistic reign of his son Shallum, God said: "Does it make you a king to have more and more cedar? Did not your father have food and drink? He did what was right and just, so all went well with him. He defended the cause of the poor and needy, and so all went well. Is that not what it means to know me?" (Jeremiah 22:15-16).

The covenant community is to be a community of compassion. Jesus underscored this emphasis on mercy when He said, "Blessed are the merciful, for they will be shown mercy" (Matthew 5:7).

Of course, this covenant principle applies to both men and women. And it will take the unique efforts of both men and women to do this work. But this book is about women, and a piercing, passionate question runs deep in my soul. What will happen if Christian women are motivated and activated by a covenant understanding of community and compassion and a clear concept of biblical womanhood to infuse community and compassion into our homes, churches, and communities? I know what happened in two instances, and it is truly spectacular.

NINETEENTH-CENTURY EXAMPLE

In 1866 a Presbyterian pastor was riding on horseback in the Allegheny Mountains of southwestern Virginia. He came upon a one-room, dirt-floored log cabin. Hearing that a poor sick woman lived there, he stopped to pray for her. On the first Lord's Day after she was well, Nancy McGlocklin walked six miles round trip to the minister's church. A few months later, at age forty-seven, she joined the church.

Nancy could not read, but her longing to read the Bible prompted her to join a children's Sunday school class. When she learned to read, someone gave her a Bible. It is said that she carried it to church every Sunday wrapped in a handkerchief. The pastor said she always opened it and followed along as he preached.

Nancy took her children to church and was soon also taking several other mountain children on the six-mile hike. In time, she had the joy of seeing her children and her husband come into a relationship with the Savior and join the church. Her pastor said that with Nancy duties never clashed. She found a way to care for her own house and to go from house to house in that mountain region sharing her Savior with those around her. Incredible things happened.

Social life in her community improved. Drunkenness and profanity, Sabbath-breaking, and all kinds of open sin began to disappear. The people began talking of their desire for the preaching of God's Word in their community. Nancy informed her pastor, and soon the little community was gathering each Sunday afternoon under a beautiful oak tree that the children called "our church." When winter came, the group moved to an old house. Here many were led to the Savior and continue to be led to Him, for this is now the Seven Springs Presbyterian Church in Glade Spring, Virginia.

An article in the 1903 *Christian Observer* said that few who knew that community in 1875 would have recognized it ten years later. "Dilapidated houses had been put in good order, fences repaired or built anew, paint and whitewash freely used, the lands cleaned up and planted with crops, and people, Sunday by Sunday, assembled in the church, wearing clothes that became the Lord's Day and their incomes."[2]

In 1886 the minister, who had retired, visited his old church. While sitting in the home of one of his former flock talking about the happy changes that had taken place, he asked, "How has it all come about?"

The answer came from an old bedridden woman: "Nancy done it all."

"How could she do such a work as this?" the minister asked.

"She goes everywhere in this mountain and never leaves no cabin without saying a word for Jesus," was the response.

Nancy McGlocklin had no grand social agenda. She had no extraordinary opportunities. She did not seek power or recognition. I am confident that never in her wildest dreams did she imagine her story being recorded in a book in the latter part of the twentieth century. But I don't think it would have made any difference. I think that if Nancy could have peeped through the corridors of time, she would have done exactly what she did. Nancy was a pilgrim with an eternal perspective. Her mountain community was a dry place, but she made it an oasis.

I think I am so smitten with this story for three reasons.

First, Nancy understood the centrality of the church in her Christian life. Her spiritual growth took place in the church, and her ministries flowed from the church to the community.

Second, Nancy started with her own family. Apparently, her faith did not come between Nancy and her husband. Her family was her ministry.

The third reason I am smitten is that most of us are like Nancy. We don't live in log cabins with dirt floors, but we are ordinary women living ordinary lives. But the extraordinary reality is that because we are redeemed daughters of the King, there are eternal repercussions to our obedience beyond our wildest imaginations.

I am saddened by this story because "Nancy done it all." That's not the way it should be. But wait—obviously others joined her, because a church was formed. Perhaps the old woman meant that Nancy started it all. I like that! That is as it should be.

Nancy was a channel of compassion, and thus she became a catalyst for compassion. The results were pretty amazing. The culture of her community was radically transformed even to this day through the continuing influence of Seven Springs Church.

A TWENTIETH-CENTURY EXAMPLE

Loving the sinner and hating the sin is easy to say but hard to do. The church I am privileged to be a member of walked this spiritual tightrope without compromising mercy or truth. The issue was homosexuality.

Our county commissioners passed a resolution saying that homosexuality is not consistent with the values of our county. Many local churches, including our own, supported this resolution. The brouhaha instigated by the militant "gay rights" groups received copious coverage from the media. "Hatemongers" was one of the nicer labels given to local pastors.

During the very time that our church was taking an unwavering position against homosexuality, Anne shared at our women's Bible study that her son Miles had AIDS. I will never forget the immediate response. With no hesitation every woman in the room rose and surrounded Anne with tears, hugs, and love. Over the next twenty-one months this community of compassion enfolded its arms around this young man and his parents as they lovingly received him back into their home and cared for him. The pastors and elders faithfully prayed for and ministered to Miles, but I asked Anne to tell me how women were channels of compassion to him. Her reflections poignantly portray woman's capacity for practical expressions of compassion.

"One woman communicated a tender love to Miles by writing him several times every week. When his eyesight failed, she brought the beauty of God's creation to him by painting wonderful word pictures of the scenes she saw in her own yard. She even wrote when she was out of town.

"Another woman brought flowers, and another loaned her eyes to Miles and regularly read to him. She also sat on the front steps and cried with me.

"As Miles required more care, and I became more weary, women were mobilized to bring in meals on a regular basis. Next to the prayers, this was the greatest ministry, because it continued so faithfully over an extended period of time. What a bond of love it formed as these women lovingly came into our home week after week.

"The outpouring of love was palpable. It sustained us, and it was used of the Lord to break through to Miles. Before his death, he embraced the Savior whose body embraced him with such authentic love.

"Miles's physical and spiritual struggles were intense to the very end. I am grateful that he did not suffer alone. And neither did we. The body of Christ mourned with us at his death, but not as those who mourn without hope. As the chorus of a song Miles loved to listen to in the final days of his life says: "If you could see me now/I'm walking streets of gold."

I had asked Anne to wait until last to tell me about Judy. I knew that Judy's ministry had been profound. When I said, "Now tell me about Judy," Anne could not contain her emotion. Words failed, and tears flowed as she reflected on Judy's phenomenal ministry of compassion.

"Judy's first visits were just to drop in for a few minutes. Then she started coming to talk to Miles about the Lord. Soon she came and went in our home as a member of the family. She brought food, flowers, special treats as Miles's appetite began to wane, and she drove us to appointments when he became wheelchair bound and I was growing weak from fatigue. It had always been difficult for me to accept help, much less ask for it. With Judy I didn't have to ask. She anticipated our needs. Her extravagant love earned her the credibility to be very direct in her conversations with Miles about his need for a Savior. She fought many spiritual battles with us, but she shared in the victory of seeing Miles come to faith in Jesus."

I, too, could not think of Judy without the tears flowing. Part of the beauty of her intense ministry was that it had not been carried out in a vacuum. She was the daily arms and legs of our entire congregation in that situation, and the covenant community supported her in prayer and in expressions of encouragement. As she entered into this spiritual battleground, the elders of the church and many women covered her and her family in prayer.

Compassion is a community affair. In a practical sense, everyone does not do everything; but in a spiritual sense we do. God called particular ones out for this ministry to Miles, even as others were called out for other ministries. But when one member of the body acts, we all act.

These are stunning examples of women being channels of compassion, but sometimes channels get clogged.

A CLOGGED CHANNEL

There are many things that clog the channel of compassion: anger, unforgiveness, a root of bitterness, emotional pain, lack of confidence, and on and on the list goes. Some women even say the men in their lives are the deterrent.

But the truth is, no person or thing can clog our channel; we do that to ourselves. The ugly guck that clogs the channel is sin—not someone else's sin but our own. Our little girls pout and whine when they don't get their way, and so do we.

Women often allow past experiences and current circumstances to restrain them. But in God's economy, these situations are actually the setting to learn how to rejoice with those who rejoice and weep with those who weep. As God's compassionate grace sweeps over us, it compels us to move toward those who cause us pain. As "the Father of compassion and the God of all comfort" comforts us in our troubles, we are equipped to "comfort those in any trouble with the comfort we ourselves have received from God" (2 Corinthians 1:3-4).

Women often feel that men are the obstacle. When we become aware of a need and have to wait for men to allocate the funds or approve the plans, their deliberations and investigations seem laborious and uncaring. But God designed us differently, and these differences give wonderful balance to the ministry of compassion. Satan pulls out all the stops to stymie us by pitting men and women against each other in compassion-work, because compassion is an essential part of the covenant community's authenticity before the world. The gender gap is sin-inspired; gender-partnering is God-inspired.

Rather than seeing people or circumstances as obstacles to compassion, it seems that God is calling us to see them as opportunities to learn compassion. An unclogged channel will flow first toward the people and situations in our lives that appear to be the obstruction, and then with God's blessing it will flow unhindered and unpolluted onto a hurting world.

UNCLOGGING THE CHANNEL

The enemy of compassion is neither circumstances nor people. Satan is the one trying to derail us, but we are the only ones who can obstruct the free flow of compassion. This is a choice we make. Circumstances and people may redirect the flow of compassion, but nothing can stop that stream except our own sinful stubbornness.

Unclogging the channel requires repentance.

What is repentance? The Westminster Shorter Catechism responds: "Repentance unto life is a saving grace, whereby a sinner, out of a true sense of his sin, and apprehension of the mercy of God in Christ, doth, with grief and hatred of his sin, turn from it unto God, with full purpose of, and endeavor after, new obedience."[3]

Or in the words of The Catechism for Young Children, repentance means: "To hate and forsake sin because it is displeasing to God."[4]

Covenant community and compassion swell as we hate and forsake our sin because it displeases our God. It is our sin that keeps us from His presence, and it is His presence that empowers us to cultivate community and to be channels of compassion. Community and compassion are persuasive evidences of our identification with Him.

IN SUMMARY

When Moses asked to see God's glory, God said He would put Moses in a cleft in the rock and cover him with His hand, because if Moses saw God, he would die. But God agreed to remove His hand so that Moses could see His back. Then God came down in a cloud. "And he passed in front of Moses, proclaiming, 'The Lord, the Lord, the compassionate and gracious God, slow to anger, abounding in love and faithfulness, maintaining love to thousands, and forgiving wickedness, rebellion and sin . . . '" (Exodus 34:5-7).

God revealed His glory by proclaiming His compassion. And so do we.

The true woman will unselfishly unleash "the springs of mercy" in her heart by being a channel of His compassion. This reflection of God's glory will bring joy to Him and comfort to His people.

Personal Reflection

1. Read Isaiah 53 and 54 and meditate on God's compassion toward you. Record your thoughts in your journal.

2. Make a list of any past or current circumstances that are clog-

ging your channel of compassion. Then ask God to show you any sinful responses you have toward those circumstances and to give you repenting grace.

3. Do you view the men in your life as obstacles to compassion? If so, ask God for repenting grace and for wisdom to know how to partner with men in compassion-work.

4. Ask God if there is any way that He wants you to be a channel of His compassion. Perhaps a visit to a nursing home, a meal to a sick neighbor, an invitation for dinner to a widow, enfolding a single into your family, or a note of encouragement to one who has offended you is the opportunity He has placed before you.

5. Meet with some other women from your church and talk about what ministries of mercy you are currently doing. Pray about other ways you can collectively demonstrate compassion in your church and community. Talk and pray about how you can offer assistance to the deacons in your church in their ministries of mercy.

PART THREE

ℋER VIRTUE

Are the virtues of piety, purity, domesticity,

and submissiveness biblical virtues?

If they are biblical virtues, how do we

incorporate them into our lives?

❧

MY PRAYER

That as we study the lives of women we meet on the pages of Scripture, you will be challenged by their moments of triumph and warned by their moments of failure.

❧

MY CHALLENGE

"Therefore, as God's chosen people, holy and dearly loved, clothe yourselves with compassion, kindness, humility, gentleness and patience. Bear with each other and forgive whatever grievances you may have against one another. Forgive as the Lord forgave you. And over all these virtues put on love, which binds them all together in perfect unity."

— COLOSSIANS 3:12-14

❧

$\mathcal{D}$ IVORCE

If someone had told me on my wedding day that my marriage would end in divorce, I would not have believed them. Divorce was not in our family vocabulary. But ten years of living with alcohol finally dealt a death blow to my marriage.

As I look back, I realize that my husband probably had a serious drinking problem before we married. We met at church, and in my naivete, I never suspected a problem. We were both from Christian homes, he had a seemingly solid commitment to Christ, and it never entered my mind that we would have anything other than a loving Christian home. Within a year I knew that things were not right, but when I asked if he had been drinking, he denied it. For the next seven years I vacillated between suspicion, denial, fear, and anger. My embarrassment led to elaborate attempts to cover for him. I now realize that I actually enabled his drinking.

Why would I engage in such destructive behavior? In addition to ignorance of alcohol, I was afraid of the future. We had two children, and I could not face the possibility of having to return to work if this marriage failed. I also felt that to abandon the marriage would be sinful. Woven through all of this were his controlling schemes to convince me that I could never make it without him, that his temper was my fault, and that I had no biblical grounds to leave him.

I finally broke and went to my pastor's wife for spiritual guidance. She explained that when a woman cannot trust the protection and authority of her husband, she should look to the elders of her church. She told me that this was not a quick or easy solution, but that it was the right thing to do.

Over the next months the elders worked with my husband and me, but the drinking persisted. My husband had been unemployed for two years. We were not in immediate financial crisis, but in many ways this was another enabler. When his drunken rages became more violent, a trial separation was arranged in order to protect the children and me. It was hoped that this would motivate him to get treatment for his drinking.

The elders tried valiantly to get my husband to assume his responsibilities, but eventually the money was depleted, and I had to assume all responsibility for our family. The day came when the elders determined that I had been deserted, and there were biblical grounds for divorce.

I feel intense sadness over the death of this marriage and great pity for this man who is a slave to alcohol. I know the physical pain of a broken heart. But the part of this story that I want to shout from the rooftop is the absolute truth of God's promise: "My grace is sufficient for you, for my power is made perfect in weakness" (2 Corinthians 12:9).

Let me share some of the ways God kept this promise to me.

First, he sent a friend to walk every step of the path with me. She listened to me, cried with me, and prayed for me. She went with me when I met with the elders and the attorney. I could tell her my every thought, and she kept loving me. She sat with me in church, went out to eat with me on Friday nights, stayed with me when the children were with their dad, and made me laugh at crazy moments. She kept me sane.

Second, God gave me faithful and diligent elders who were not afraid to do the tough work of shepherding. They helped me financially until I could get a job; they lovingly explained things to my children; they prayed and prayed and prayed. And they continue to pray. They also continue to try to fill the void in my children's lives by giving them that male attention and affirmation that is so needed.

Third, God showered His grace on me through the elder's wife who was assigned to disciple me through this process. At our first meeting she gave me a journal and encouraged me to record my journey. She explained the urgency of spending time with the Lord each day. My Bible and my journal were my lifeline over the next few months, and they continue to be my daily companions in my pilgrimage. When the separation began, my stress level was so high that I was on an emotional roller coaster. Many days I did not see or feel God's presence, but I knew He was there. As the entries below show, journaling helped me to stay focused on Him and His Word. These entries begin with the separation.

April 21: "Let not your heart be troubled. . . . " My heart is heavy and sad today. I feel unstable. My prayer is that my heart will not be troubled and that I will focus on the Lord.

April 22: I thought it would be hard to go to church alone today, but God met my need through loving brothers and sisters in Christ. An elder and his wife opened their home and invited the children and me for lunch.

April 29: The Lord is dealing with me about judging others and about my temper. I asked Him to show me myself, and He opened my eyes to some ugly sin. I have been so focused on my husband's sin that I tend not to see myself as I really am. I pray that God will forgive me and help me turn from my sin.

May 2: Today I had a pity party. I felt lonely, uncertain, and sad. My heaviest burden is how the children are doing—what are they really thinking? I feel cheated for them because they haven't had the experience of having a daddy who was there for them. Even as I write this, I realize that God can fill this void in their lives by His presence—that is my prayer.

May 4: "Never will I leave you; never will I forsake you" (Hebrew 13:5). It is so reassuring to me to know that even at a time of uncertainty God will not leave me.

May 22: "You will grieve, but your grief will turn to joy. . . . and no one will take away your joy" (John 16:20, 22). I hold on to this promise.

May 24: "The Lord is close to the brokenhearted" (Psalm 34:18). I feel God's closeness. I trust Him for my needs and pray that He will help me to forgive my husband.

June 4: "Out of the depths I cry to you, O Lord; O Lord, hear my voice. Let your ears be attentive to my cry for mercy" (Psalm 130:1-2). My Lord cares when I feel like a failure. He smiles and gives me gentle words of encouragement. Thank you, Lord!

June 27: "Therefore we do not lose heart. Though outwardly we are wasting away, yet inwardly we are being renewed day by day" (2 Corinthians 4:16). Though I feel in limbo, it is such an encouragement to know that inwardly I'm being renewed day by day.

June 28: My pastor's wife and I met with a woman whose father was an alcoholic. I shed many tears, but she helped me so much. Some suggestions that I must remember: Make sure the children understand that their dad has a drinking problem and that it is neither their fault nor my fault and that none of us can "fix" it. Remember that they are part of a covenant community and don't be afraid to ask supportive males to spend time with them. Keep assuring them of God's love. Pray with and for them about their dad. Go to other adults, and not the children, for my emotional support. Pray that I will have a forgiving spirit and that the children will see this in me. Watch for signs of perfectionism or rebellion, since they may tend to go to one of these extremes. Don't overcompensate for what is happening to them. Keep them involved in church life so they will have a strong sense of belonging to the covenant community.

July 9: Money is short this month, and I found myself worrying frantically. I asked God to provide, began paying the bills, and there was just enough to cover them.

July 31: "Trust in the Lord with all your heart and lean not on your own understanding. In all your ways acknowledge him, and he will make your paths straight" (Proverbs 3:5-6). This says it all. Help me, Lord, to do this.

August 26: I feel overwhelmed with the job search. I have been out of the job market so long, and I lack the skills I need. I must trust the Lord.

Sept. 14: Praise the Lord! I was offered a job today. The woman said there were other people more qualified, but she felt she should offer it to me. I know this is from the Lord.

The Lord continues to be my sufficiency. My children and I have adjusted to our new life, and I daily trust Him to care for us. I am grateful for His church and for the privilege of being a part of His covenant family. The Lord has given me a deep burden for other women going through what I have been through, and already He is giving me opportunities to walk with them through their pain and to help them hold on to God's promises.

I'm not saying my life is easy. I am exhausted! It's difficult to give up being a stay-at-home mom. It's hard to attend functions alone. It breaks my heart that my children don't have a wonderful father like I had. But God gives me strength and wisdom to continue living for Him. Romans 8:26-28 is one of my anchors. It's comforting to know that when I hurt so much and don't know what to pray, the Holy Spirit intercedes for me; and it's reassuring to know that God works for the good of those who love Him.

—Name withheld

CHAPTER
SEVEN

$\mathscr{P}$IETY

*Female piety is the best, the only sincere expression of
female gratitude to God. An irreligious woman is also an
ungrateful one. She who loves not Christ, whomsoever
else she may love, and however chaste and pure that love
may be, is living immeasurably below her obligations,
and has a stain of guilt upon her heart and her con-
science, which no other virtue can efface or conceal.*

Female Piety

Piety, purity, domesticity, and submissiveness: provocative, red-flag words. Our task is to see if these principal virtues of the nineteenth-century concept of the true woman are cultural virtues of a particular time and place or if they are biblical virtues that transcend time and place.

To tackle this task, our starting point will be Proverbs 31. Then we will illustrate each virtue by spotlighting a woman in Scripture. The scrutiny of the spotlight may be uncomfortable, both for our sisters from antiquity and for ourselves. But if these virtues are in fact true, noble, right, pure, lovely, admirable, excellent, or praiseworthy, we are obliged to "think about such things" (Philippians 4:8).

VIRTUES CLARIFICATION

William Bennett's bestseller *The Book of Virtues* brought that word back into vogue. I love the book. When our grandchildren visit, they ask for the "please, please story" or "Diamonds and Toads."

In the introduction to the book, Bennett says that it

> . . . is intended to aid in the time-honored task of the moral education of the young. . . . This book, then, is a "how-to" book for moral literacy. If we want our children to possess the traits of character we most admire, we need to teach them what those traits are and why they deserve both admiration and allegiance. . . . the vast majority of Americans share a respect for certain fundamental traits of character: honesty, compassion, courage, and perseverance. These are virtues. But because children are not born with this knowledge, they need to learn what these virtues are.[1]

I could not agree more. But this is not what I am talking about. The virtues I am talking about go beyond moral excellence. Oswald Chambers explains it in *My Utmost for His Highest*.

> Our Lord never patches up our natural virtues. He re- makes the whole man on the inside. . . . The life God plants in us develops its own virtues, not the virtues of Adam, but of Jesus Christ. Watch how God will wither up your confidence in natural virtues after sanctification, and in any power you have, until you learn to draw your life from the reservoir of the resurrection life of Jesus. Thank God if you are going through a drying-up experience!
>
> . . . God does not build up our natural virtues and transfig- ure them, because our natural virtues can never come any- where near what Jesus Christ wants. No natural love, no natural patience, no natural purity can ever come up to His demands. But as we bring every bit of our bodily life into har- mony with the new life which God has put in us, He will exhibit in us the virtues that were characteristic of the Lord Jesus.[2]

Biblical virtues cannot be learned from a how-to book. These character qualities are evidences of grace. They are responses of obedience that flow from a new heart. And a new heart is a gift from God to His covenant children.

"I will give you a new heart and put a new spirit in you; I will remove from you your heart of stone and give you a heart of flesh. And I will put my Spirit in you and move you to follow my decrees and be careful to keep my laws. You will live in the land I gave your forefathers; you will be my people, and I will be your God" (Ezekiel 36:26-28).

A stony heart can learn, admire, and ascribe to "fundamental traits of character" that we all agree are commendable. But only a heart of flesh can keep God's laws, for " . . . without faith it is impossible to please God, because anyone who comes to him must believe that he exists and that he rewards those who earnestly seek him" (Hebrews 11:6).

THE VIRTUOUS WOMAN

Any mention of the Proverbs 31 woman and most of us go into a tailspin of self-imposed guilt or indignant rationalization. And single women often say, "That has nothing to do with me; it is about being a wife, and I am not one."

Granted the behaviors mentioned in Proverbs 31, just as the ones listed in Titus 2, are examples from the life of a married woman. But the Proverbs 31 profile begins with a mother posing the question to her son: "Who can find a virtuous woman?" (KJV). She then describes for him the benefits of marrying a woman of noble character. Whereas the description of how a virtuous woman behaves in her marriage may not be applicable to a single woman, the goal of a noble character does apply.

Proverbs 31 reaches it zenith with these words: "Charm is deceptive and beauty is fleeting; but a woman who fears the Lord is to be praised."

This perspective of womanhood is one every Christian woman should grab and cling to tenaciously. We are inundated with deformed, debilitating views of womanhood. This image is refreshing and realistic for the woman of biblical faith. Whatever her age, appearance, or situation, this woman is ultimately one who fearlessly fears the Lord. The word translated fear does not mean terror. It means to reverence, to stand in awe.

The psalmist tells us that "The fear of the Lord is the beginning of wisdom; all who follow his precepts have good understanding" (Psalm 111:10).

Wisdom is the link between fear of the Lord and a virtuous life.

The Hebrew word for wise, *hakam*, means more than knowledge or intelligence. It means the right use of knowledge. It involves a way of thinking about and reacting to life's experiences. The wisdom of the Old Testament is a worldview that differs from other ancient worldviews because it reflects the teaching of a personal God who is holy, righteous, and just and who expects those living in covenant relationship with Him to reflect His character in the practical affairs of life.

Wisdom begins with a reverential awe of God as He is revealed in Scripture. This opens the way to view the world and our place in it through the lens of God's revealed will. The more we see life through this lens, the clearer our perception of how to live out God's principles in daily life.

Charm and beauty may entice for a season, but reverence for God produces wisdom that yields a lifestyle of virtue. And this lifestyle elicits lasting praise.

PURITAN PIETY

I know that *piety* is an old-fashioned word. But it is time that we dusted it off and rediscovered its rich meaning. I confess that it is a reach for me to write about it because I am so unfamiliar with it conceptually and experientially. I want to be more mature in my faith, but when I read of the piety of the Puritans, I know that I am so immature. I feel like a spiritual wimp.

The Greek word *eusebeo* means to reverence. It is akin to *eusebes*, which is sometimes translated pious, devout, or godly.

In his *Institutes*, John Calvin says:

> The gist of true piety does not consist in a fear which would gladly flee the judgment of God, but . . . rather in a pure and true zeal which loves God altogether as Father, and reveres him truly as Lord, embraces his justice and dreads to offend him more than to die. . . . I call "piety" that reverence joined with love of God which the knowledge of his benefits induces. For until men recognize that they owe everything to God, that they are nourished by his fatherly care, that he is the Author of their every good, that they should seek nothing beyond him—they will never yield him willing service. Nay, unless they establish their complete happiness in him, they will never give themselves truly and sincerely to him.[3]

J. I. Packer says that four qualities characterize Puritan piety:

> The first is *humility*, the cultivated lowliness of a sinful creature who is always in the presence of a great and holy God, and can only live before him through being constantly pardoned. The second is *receptivity* . . . openness to be taught, corrected, and directed by one's discoveries in Scripture . . . disciplined by the darkness of disappointment . . . encouraged by happy providences . . . readiness to believe that the good hand of a faithful and gracious God, who is ripening his children for future glory, shapes it all. . . . The third is *doxology*, the passion to turn everything into worship and so to glorify God by all one's words and deeds. The fourth is *energy*, the spiritual energy of the true Protestant work ethic whereby laziness and passivity are damned as irreligious, just because so much remains to be done before God's name is hallowed in his world as it should be. That all four qualities are formed by the Puritan view of God . . . is obvious . . . they constitute a mind- and heart-set which, once formed, nothing can daunt or destroy. . . .[4]

Packer goes on to explain that "in mapping the path of piety," the Puritans emphasized four areas:

> ... the first steps (conviction and conversion through faith and repentance ...); the fight (against the world, the flesh, and the devil ...); the fellowship (communion with God ... and with other Christians); and the finish (dying well, in faith and hope, with all preparations made and a clear and quiet conscience as one moves into that final momentous meeting with the Father and the Son).[5]

It is no wonder that Puritan piety penetrated the soul, the family, the church, and the culture.

FEMALE PIETY

The call to piety is not gender-specific, but the expression of piety is sometimes colored by gender. This must be the reason the nineteenth-century preacher wrote a book titled *Female Piety*. He surely was not implying that males were exempt from piety. But I fear we have lost this distinction. We have inhaled the feminist notion that there are no gender distinctions.

Alexis de Tocqueville made some startling observations on gender:

> There are people in Europe who, confounding together the different characteristics of the sexes, would make man and woman into beings not only equal but alike. They would give to both the same functions, impose on both the same duties, and grant to both the same rights; they would mix them in all things—their occupations, their pleasures, their business. It may readily be conceived that by thus attempting to make one sex equal to the other, both are degraded, and from so preposterous a medley of the works of nature nothing could ever result but weak men and disorderly

women. . . . [The Americans] admit that as nature has appointed such wide differences between the physical and moral constitution of man and woman, her manifest design was to give a distinct employment to their various faculties; and they hold that improvement does not consist in making beings so dissimilar do pretty nearly the same things, but in causing each of them to fulfill their respective tasks in the best possible manner.[6]

There is a difference between encouraging female piety and in feminizing piety. Often women tell me that their husbands or the men in their church are not spiritual. Many pastors make the same observation. This makes me wonder if we are putting a female spin on how spirituality should be expressed. It also makes me wonder if we have unintentionally accepted the feminist lie that female is better. To insist that men verbalize or socialize their faith in the way women do is to demean their maleness. When Christian men responsibly provide for their families, attend church on Sundays, love their wives and children, and give their offerings to the Lord, we should celebrate their male spirituality. I am convinced that women would never have done the tedious, technical work of drafting The Westminster Confession of Faith, but I suspect there were women who were praying every day those men were debating. The church is richer because of the different expressions of piety.

We must neither demean male piety nor dismiss female piety. Like the author of *Female Piety*, we should challenge women to "rise to the true dignity of your nature by rising into the region of true religion. Consume not your life in pursuits, innocent it may be, but frivolous and unworthy of your powers, your destiny, and your duty. . . . Behold an existence opening before you, which you may fill with the sanctity, bliss, and honour of a Christian, as well as with all the virtues of a woman. Withdraw your heart from vanity, and consecrate it to piety."[7]

Elizabeth Prentiss provides an example of female piety. Her husband writes:

> Elizabeth's early Christian character, although largely shaped by that of her father, was also, like his, vitally affected by the religious spirit and methods then dominant. Several distinct elements entered into the piety of New England at that period. . . . There was, first of all, the old Puritan element which the Pilgrim Fathers and their immediate successors brought with them from the mother-country, and which had been nourished by the writings of the great Puritan divines of the seventeenth century. . . . This lay at the foundation of the whole structure, giving it strength, solidity, earnestness, and power.[8]

We see this spiritual vitality in her letters and journal entries:

> *August 25, 1840:* I am beginning to feel that I have enough to do without looking out for a great, wide place in which to work, and to appreciate the simple lines:
>
> > *"The trivial round, the common task,*
> > *Would furnish all we ought to ask;*
> > *Room to deny ourselves; a road*
> > *To bring us daily nearer God."*
>
> Those words "daily nearer God" have an inexpressible charm for me. I long for such nearness to Him that all other objects shall fade into comparative insignificance—so that to have a thought, a wish, a pleasure apart from Him shall be impossible.[9]
>
> *June 3, 1871:* The experience of the past winter would impress upon me the fact that place and position have next to nothing to do with happiness; that we can be wretched in a palace, radiant in a dungeon.[10]

In a letter to a young friend in 1873, she speaks of prayer as "the greatest favor one friend can render another," and then adds:

> But perhaps I may put one beyond it—Christian example. I ought to be so saintly, so consecrated, that you could not be with me and not catch the very spirit of heaven; never get a letter from me that did not quicken your steps in the divine life. But while I believe the principle of love to Christ is entrenched in the depths of my soul, the emotion of love is not always in that full play I want it to be. No doubt He judges us by the principle He sees to exist in us, but we can't help judging ourselves, in spite of ourselves, by our feelings. At church this morning my mind kept wandering to and fro; I thought of you about twenty times; thought about my flowers; thought of 501 things; and then got up and sang, "I love Thy kingdom, Lord," as if I cared for that and nothing else. What He has to put up with in me! But I believe in Him, I love Him, I hate everything in my soul and in my life that is unlike Him. I hope the confession of my shortcomings won't discourage you; it is no proof that at my age you will not be far beyond such weakness and folly as often carry me away captive. . . . As far as earthly blessings go I am as near perfect happiness as a human being can be; everything is heaped on me. What I want is more of Christ, and that is what I hope you pray that I may have.[11]

I feel as if she is inside my skin! She says what I think and feel. And she said it over a hundred years ago. But there is another woman who, I suspect, thought and felt the same things over two thousand years ago.

A PICTURE OF PIETY

The home of Simon the leper in the village of Bethany was the scene of a remarkable picture of piety. Jesus and the disciples were gathered for a meal. The disciples were probably laughing and retelling stories of their experiences with Jesus. Martha was serving, and suddenly Mary did something so bizarre that everything stopped. The moment froze. And Jesus grabbed it and made it a memorial.

Mary inconspicuously maneuvered her way to the place where Jesus was reclining at the table. She broke an alabaster flask of very costly fragrant oil, poured it on his head and feet, and wiped his feet with her hair.

Suddenly all eyes were on her.

"When the disciples saw it, they were indignant. 'Why this waste?' they asked. 'This perfume could have been sold at a high price and the money given to the poor.'"

Jesus immediately came to her defense: "'Why are you bothering this woman? She has done a beautiful thing to me. The poor you will always have with you, but you will not always have me. When she poured this perfume on my body, she did it to prepare me for burial. I tell you the truth, wherever this gospel is preached throughout the world, what she has done will also be told, in memory of her'" (Matthew 26:6-13; also recorded in Mark 14:3-9 and John 12:1-8).

Mary was consumed with "that reverence joined with love of God which the knowledge of his benefits induces"—the gist of piety as Calvin said.

Try to imagine the occasion. Here is the One who had affirmed her when she sat at His feet (Luke 10) and who brought her brother Lazarus back to life (John 11). Her reverence and love for Him has grown with her deepening knowledge of Him. If she tries to contain it, she will explode. She must demonstrate her devotion. So without considering the extravagance, she hurries home and gets the perfume even though it is worth a year's wages. There is a sensitive creativity and a holy abandon about her actions. This is a female expression of piety.

I suspect that Mary hoped no one would notice, but Jesus said that "wherever this gospel is preached in the whole world" it would be told. Why would Jesus call such attention to this act and couple it to the proclamation of the Gospel?

I think it must be that this is a stunning picture of the result of the transforming power of the Gospel.

There are three things I think we can learn from Mary about piety.

First, Jesus said, "she has done a beautiful thing to me." I must admit that I love doing works of ministry. The thrill of projects and programs and people is exhilarating. And too often I realize I am doing it for that reason. True piety does it for Jesus, regardless of recognition or results.

Second, we hear a lot about counting the cost of discipleship, and well we should. But there are times when our love for Jesus is so intense there is no cost that matters. We do not always live in that intensity. Indeed our mortal bodies could not bear such ongoing force. But it is those extraordinary moments that give spiritual vitality to the ordinary moments of our lives. True piety remembers those moments and draws upon them to make the common and the routine moments sacred.

Third, Mary had to break an expensive vase to anoint Jesus. It is often through brokenness that the perfume of grace gives its sweetest fragrance. Brokenness is a passage to piety.

A PASSAGE TO PIETY

It seems to me that today we think of brokenness coming through difficult circumstances, and surely that is one way the Lord presses us to Himself. But when I look at Scripture, it seems that it was not circumstances but awareness of sin that evoked brokenness. The more we know God, the more we know of our own sinfulness, and the more we reverence Him. The classic example is Isaiah.

> . . . I saw the Lord seated on a throne, high and exalted, and
> the train of his robe filled the temple. Above him were seraphs,
> each with six wings: With two wings they covered their faces,

with two they covered their feet, and with two they were fly-
ing. And they were calling to one another:

> *"Holy, holy, holy is the Lord Almighty;*
> *the whole earth is full of his glory."*

At the sound of their voices the doorposts and thresholds
shook and the temple was filled with smoke.

This knowledge of the holiness of God caused Isaiah to
exclaim:

"Woe to me!" I cried. "I am ruined! For I am a man of unclean
lips, and I live among a people of unclean lips, and my eyes
have seen the King, the Lord Almighty"
— Isaiah 6:1-5

At this point of brokenness when Isaiah realized his sinfulness,
the seraph flew to him, touched his mouth with a live coal, and
said:

"See, this has touched your lips; your guilt is taken away and
your sin atoned for."

Then things took a dramatic upward turn.

Then I heard the voice of the Lord saying, "Whom shall
I send? And who will go for us?" And I said, "Here am I.
Send me!"

And God did.

When we see God as He shows us Himself in the Bible, we will
behold His majesty and His holiness, and like Isaiah we will cry
out, "Woe is me!" In this brokenness God touches us with His
grace.

Mary's willingness to break the costly vase came from her

knowledge of Jesus. The passage to piety is brokenness over our sin, but the passage begins with a true knowledge of God and ends with true obedience to Him.

I am not speaking here about the initial awareness of our sin at conversion. I am talking about sanctification: "the work of God's free grace, whereby we are renewed in the whole man after the image of God, and are enabled more and more to die unto sin, and live unto righteousness."[12]

PURSUING PIETY

Assurance of salvation and complacency about salvation are two different things. The Puritans had great assurance, but they were never complacent about their salvation. This is why so many were diligent in keeping journals of their spiritual pilgrimage. They did not want to lose the lessons God taught them through trials. They did not want to forget God's mercies. They wanted to recognize their sin so they could die to it. The Puritans realized that their chief adversary was not Satan, but self, so they kept a watchful eye on their souls.

Journaling helps us to concentrate on our communion with God, and the Puritans knew the value of this kind of meditation. J. I. Packer writes:

> This rational, resolute, passionate piety was conscientious without becoming obsessive, law-oriented without lapsing into legalism, and expressive of Christian liberty without any shameful lurches into license. . . . Knowing also the dishonesty and deceitfulness of fallen human hearts, they . . . examined themselves regularly for spiritual blind spots and lurking inward evils. They may not be called morbid or introspective on this account, however; on the contrary, they found the discipline of self-examination by Scripture . . . followed by the discipline of confessing and forsaking sin and renewing one's

gratitude to Christ for his pardoning mercy, to be a source of great inner peace and joy.[13]

The result was a robust and lively faith that permeated all of life.

How often we want Jesus to fix our problems, and what we should want is Jesus. Think back to the conversations I listed in chapter 2 with Christian women who became self-focused as they considered their situations. When we are faced with difficult conditions, if only we would consider them pure joy, knowing that "the testing of your faith develops perseverance. Perseverance must finish its work so that you may be mature and complete, not lacking anything" (James 1:2-4).

If only we would look at our initial response, realize that we have succumbed to our adversary self, and cry out with David, "Have mercy on me, O God, according to your unfailing love; according to your great compassion blot out my transgressions. Wash away all my iniquity and cleanse me from my sin" (Psalm 51: 1-2).

If only we, like Isaiah, would cry out, "Woe is me!"

Then we would feel the flaming touch of grace on our lives and hear the Master's call to serve Him.

And then we would not be able to contain our love. It would be poured out in humility and in service for Him.

IN SUMMARY

Piety is a biblical virtue. It is an intentional, energetic, integration of faith into all of life in order to glorify the Lord. It is a virtue to be pursued by all Christian women. It is a legitimate mark of the true woman in all places and times.

There are no shortcuts to piety. There is no instant holiness. The basics of Bible study, prayer, meditation, fasting, repentance, corporate worship, participation in the community of faith, and courageous obedience are the stuff of true piety. This is the stuff of a mature faith. Theological principles and tender practice must be wedded.

The true woman will unleash her God-given femininity in expressing her love for Jesus with a holy abandon.

Personal Reflection

1. Pray Psalm 63:1-8 every day for a week. Memorize this passage.

2. In your journal, list the four qualities of Puritan piety: humility, receptivity, doxology, and energy. Ask God for wisdom to examine your own life in light of these qualities.

3. Read Isaiah 6:1-8 and write a prayer asking God to confront you with your own sin and to break you.

4. Read Matthew 26:6-13 and pray about how you can demonstrate your love for Jesus with a holy abandon.

ℋANDICAPPED

My journey with the Savior had been a journey of joy from my conversion during junior high school in Ohio, through high school in Florida and college at Clemson University, to my marriage in 1979. Then came the summer of 1982 when, for a time, that joy was extinguished.

Our firstborn, Jessica, had struggled a bit in her first three months of life, but her doctor had expressed no great concern. That summer, however, while her pediatrician was away and Jessica had some trouble, another doctor told us quite bluntly that he believed she had cerebral palsy. Though he was wrong in the details, his observation was generally right—Jessica was not going to be like ordinary kids. Tests revealed a chromosomal anomaly that likely had occurred at conception and would leave Jessica profoundly disabled mentally and physically. From there my journey with joy became rugged, with many slips—even a free fall perhaps. I had little strength or concentration for the things I had previously loved. The cloud in my life seemed symbolized by a white sheet I put over my floor loom, a cover that blanketed my creative outlet for many months. My husband, Mike, and I both asked the inevitable "why" questions and struggled to pick up the pieces of the life we had been building, which had collapsed so suddenly.

Through the dark part of my journey, two biblical characters figured prominently in my thinking: Mary of Nazareth and Job of Uz. Mary also endured the suffering of her firstborn child. But like

Job, I have not been allowed to look behind the veil to see the reasons for my child's affliction. Mary of Nazareth, on the other hand, had an angelic visitation that told the secret of His greatness and the special nature of His life even before His birth (Luke 1:30-33). Surely she also heard from Joseph of his dream revealing another significant detail of her child's redemptive purpose (Matthew 1:20-21). She later encountered Simeon and Anna, who told her more of what to expect. Mary was forewarned that this Child would be a wonder, His life would be a blessing, and His death would be at once heartbreaking and soul-saving.

I have often wondered about Jessica's future and longed to know the purpose of her life, but no secrets have been revealed. I must wait for the scroll to be rolled back to know all the reasons for the dark threads God has woven into the tapestry of life. Mary of Nazareth knew. But whether this knowledge was good or bad, it certainly was not easy. Imagine knowing ahead of time what will happen to your child. The burden of the inevitable, especially when it involves the loss of a child, is a heavy burden indeed.

Of course, the fruit of Mary's womb from conception was perfect, the spotless Lamb. The fruit of my womb from conception was, under God's sovereign and providential hand, anything but perfect in man's eyes, but exactly what the sovereign God intended for her to be. The One, holy as His Father is holy, showed us by His holiness our brokenness and need for redemption. This other, Jessica, in her own way also reminds us of our brokenness and our need for redemption.

Though there are similarities and differences among Job, Mary, and me, we share the same conviction: we know our Redeemer lives. Job looked forward hoping in faith to see his Redeemer after his own flesh was destroyed. Mary of Nazareth looked on the face of her Redeemer throughout His earthly life. I look back through Scripture to the story and forward like Job to the prospect of being finally and fully in my Redeemer's presence. And I am confident, because of God's covenant, that with my husband and me Jessica will be among our children—whole and finally perfectly able to praise her Redeemer.

—*Mary S. Beates*
Orlando, FL

Mary Beates's husband, Mike, is an editor for *Tabletalk* magazine with Ligonier Ministries. This story is adapted, with permission, from an article in that magazine.

$\mathscr{P}$URITY

. . . a sense of excitement during religious ordinances is far less to be depended upon as a test of personal godliness, than rigid self-government, resolute will in the way of righteousness, and tender conscientiousness, exercised in obedience to the Divine authority, and under a constraining sense of the love of Christ.

Female Piety

The elaborate rituals for purification in Old Testament Israel provide a starting point for a biblical understanding of purity. These rituals vividly teach God's holiness and moral purity and our desperate need to be cleansed in order to stand in His presence.

Because the religion of Israel emphasizes so strongly the holiness of God, it develops the concept of purity with corresponding energy. The law works out a whole series of regulations. Some purifications are preparatory. They set man in a necessary state of holiness for encounter with God (Exodus 19:10; Numbers 8:15). Some are expiatory. They restore forfeited purity by lustrations (Leviticus 16:1ff.; Ezekiel 39:12; 2 Chronicles 29:15; 34:3, 8).[1] [Expiation is the covering or washing away of sin by a blood sacrifice, and lustrations are purification ceremonies.]

The Master Teacher knows the learning style of His students.

He knows that it takes concrete examples and hands-on experiences for us to grasp kingdom concepts. Old Testament rituals provide the examples and experiences needed to understand New Testament principles. The Old Testament laws and regulations for purification dramatically foreshadow the spiritual purity that is required for entrance into the kingdom and that will be reflected by citizens of the kingdom. The episode in Exodus 19 vibrates with this message.

Three months after God delivered the Israelites from bondage in Egypt, they came to Sinai. God called Moses to come up the mountain and gave him a message for the Israelites: "'You yourselves have seen what I did to Egypt, and how I carried you on eagles' wings and brought you to myself. Now if you obey me fully and keep my covenant, then out of all nations you will be my treasured possession. Although the whole earth is mine, you will be for me a kingdom of priests and a holy nation'" (Exodus 19:4-6).

Moses went down the mountain, gave the people God's message, and they responded, "'We will do everything the Lord has said.'"

Moses went back up the mountain, and the Lord said to him, "'I am going to come to you in a dense cloud, so that the people will hear me speaking with you and will always put their trust in you. . . . Go to the people and consecrate them today and tomorrow. Have them wash their clothes and be ready by the third day, because on that day the Lord will come down on Mount Sinai in the sight of all the people'" (Exodus 19:9-11).

No one can stand in the presence of the Lord God with dirty clothes. His holiness would consume us. This Old Testament ritual of washing their clothes and being ready on the third day is a picture of Jesus taking His absolutely sinless life to the cross, paying the redemption price for the sin of His people, and God showing His satisfaction with the payment by triumphantly raising Jesus from the dead on the third day. Then God puts the clothes of Jesus' righteousness on me and declares me to be pure. This is the most incredible legal transaction that has ever occurred. It was this truth that gripped Martin Luther as the words of Romans 1:17 roared in his heart: "The just shall live by faith."

POSITIONAL PURITY

The purity that is necessary for us to stand before a holy God is a forensic purity. It is a legal declaration. We are declared to be pure even while we are impure. This is not a casual dismissal of our sin. This declaration is made on the basis of the purity of Jesus being transferred to us. This is the glorious doctrine of justification. Martin Luther said that justification by faith alone is the doctrine upon which the church stands or falls. It is also the doctrine upon which we individually stand or fall.

"He was delivered over to death for our sins and was raised to life for our justification. Therefore, since we have been justified through faith, we have peace with God through our Lord Jesus Christ, through whom we have gained access by faith into this grace in which we now stand" (Romans 4:25–5:2).

When God declares us to be just, He binds Himself to us in an eternal relationship. We who had been His enemies now actually have access to Him. This is not because our clothes have been washed. Our own clothes could never be bleached enough to merit a standing before Him. We can stand in His presence because our filthy rags have been stripped from us, and we have been clothed in the perfect righteousness of Jesus. This is our assurance. This is the basis of our standing before God.

In answer to the question, "What is justification?" The Westminster Shorter Catechism responds: "Justification is an act of God's free grace, wherein He pardoneth all our sins, and accepteth us as righteous in His sight, only for the righteousness of Christ, imputed to us, and received by faith alone."[2]

Our justification is not by works; it is by faith alone. It is by Christ alone. But, as is often said, it is not a faith that is alone. The power of this transaction transforms us into "a new creation; the old is gone, the new has come!" (2 Corinthians 5:17). Purity of life does nothing to earn salvation; it is an evidence of salvation. But positional purity and practical purity are so intertwined in Scripture that they cannot and should not be unraveled. Christianity can demand a life of purity because the Christian faith makes provision for purification. As we consider the virtue of purity, it must never be separated from this provision for justification by grace through faith.

PRACTICAL PURITY

Remember the principle from chapter 7 that wisdom is the link between a fear of God and a virtuous life and that the Old Testament concept of wisdom involves a way of thinking and reacting to life's experiences. It reflects the teaching of a personal God who is holy, righteous, and just and who expects those living in covenant relationship with Him to reflect His character in the practical affairs of life.

James reinforces the idea that wisdom translates our reverence for God into our life situations: "But the wisdom that comes from heaven is first of all pure; then peace-loving, considerate, submissive, full of mercy and good fruit, impartial and sincere" (James 3:17).

The word translated pure in this verse is the Greek word *hagnos*, which means pure from defilement, not contaminated. This same word is used by John when he declares: "How great is the love the Father has lavished on us, that we should be called children of God! . . . we know that when he appears, we shall be like him, for we shall see him as he is. Everyone who has this hope in him purifies himself, just as he is pure" (1 John 3:1-3).

This is also the word used in Titus 2 where older women are told to train younger women to be pure. This is a moral and ethical purity, and women need to teach women how this is expressed in daily life. So let's put the spotlight on our Old Testament sister Miriam as she teaches us some principles of the virtue of purity. We will learn from Miriam that practical purity is passionate and oftentimes painful.

PRINCIPLES OF PURITY

To throw the spotlight on Miriam and to ignore the context of her life would be a total misrepresentation of her actions. Whenever we lift biblical characters out of the covenant framework of Scripture, we yield to self-effort moralism and end up with insipid messages of "be courageous like Esther" or "be a hard worker like Ruth" or "be whatever like whomever" with no reference to grace. As Miriam comes to center stage, remember that the story is not about her; this is the drama of redemption. This is the story of God keeping His promise to be our God and to live among us. So we must first get the big picture in view, and then we will understand Miriam's story.

Genesis tells the story of the family to whom the covenant promise had been given and ends with Joseph bringing this family to Egypt in order to provide for them. In Egypt there is a population explosion among the children of Israel, and by the opening of the book of Exodus, there is a pharaoh who neither knows nor cares about Joseph. His concern is this alien population that now outnumbers the Egyptians, so he engineers a wicked population-control scheme. All Israelite boy babies are to be killed.

It was into this cultural confusion that Jocebed's baby, the basket-child Moses, was born.

Remember, the Sovereign Director of this redemption drama is not the pharaoh; it is the Lord God. At least three plots were unfolding in the redemption drama.

First, the focus shifts from a single family (the patriarchs—Abraham, Isaac, and Jacob) to a covenant people, and someone must serve as head of that people and mediator for them. The story of Moses is much more than a tale of a brave mother who loved her baby. His life and ministry are a foreshadowing of Christ, our Head and Mediator.

In a second unfolding plot, the Israelites were a people under sentence of death. Their only hope was for God to keep His promise to save them. Baby Moses was born under the threat of death; so was the Baby Jesus. But the threat of death for Jesus was not just because of a cruel king; it was because of our sin.

The third plot is a greater revelation of God to His people. Against the background of living under a sentence of death, the Lord revealed Himself as Yahweh. At the burning bush, when Moses asked God how he should respond when the Israelites asked him the name of the one who had sent him,

> . . . God answered first, "I AM WHO I AM," then shortened it to "I AM." The name "Yahweh" ("the LORD") sounds like "I am" in Hebrew, and God finally called Himself "the LORD God of your fathers" (Exodus 3:14-16). The name in all its forms proclaims His eternal, self-sustaining, self-determining, sovereign reality—the supernatural mode of existence that the sign of the burning bush had signified (Exodus 3:2). The bush that was not consumed was God's illustration of His own inexhaustible life. In designating "Yahweh" as "My name forever" (Exodus 3:15), God indicated that His people should always think of Him as the living, reigning, powerful King that the burning bush showed Him to be.[3]

When Jocebed decided to violate the law and hide her baby, she was not just a courageous woman willing to risk her life for her child. This was a woman who put her trust in the God who had made a covenant promise to bind Himself to His people in covenant faithfulness. Jocebed was not the only woman who clung to the promise. The Hebrew midwives were pro-life crusaders who "feared God and did not do what the king of Egypt had told them to do; they let the boys live. . . . So God was kind to the midwives and the people increased and became even more numerous" (Exodus 1:17, 20).

When the baby was three months old, Jocebed could no longer hide him. She made a basket, put the baby in it, and placed it in the river. "His sister stood at a distance to see what would happen to him" (Exodus 2:4).

PASSIONATE PURITY

We are not sure how old Miriam was, but surely she was still a child herself. Why did Jocebed leave this monumental, dangerous task to her daughter? Perhaps she knew that no one would notice a young girl playing among the bushes, but a grown woman would be quite conspicuous. Whatever the reason, Jocebed's confidence in her girl-child is noteworthy, and Miriam's obedience is praiseworthy. Miriam did not live among faithless, complacent women who were unwilling to stretch the boundaries of their comfort zone. She had watched the radical, passionate purity of her mother and the midwives, and she followed their lead.

When Pharaoh's daughter came to the river to bathe, she spotted the basket and instructed her slave girl to get it. She opened the basket, saw the baby, felt sorry for him, and said, "'This is one of the Hebrew babies.'" What happened next is remarkable.

Miriam is a commentary on Proverbs 15:33: "The fear of the Lord teaches a man [a girl] wisdom.... " Young Miriam was "calm, cool, and collected," but far beyond that, she reacted with wisdom from the Lord as she skipped up to the princess and asked, "'Shall I go and get one of the Hebrew women to nurse the baby for you?'" (Exodus 2:7). There is no indication in the text that the princess had said anything about keeping the baby. Miriam's swift response to the crisis prompted this solution. Jocebed was allowed to nurse her own child and was even paid for doing it.

There must have been an intense bond between this sister and the younger brother she had risked her own life to save. When Moses was grown and had to flee after murdering the Egyptian, even the forty-year separation could not have severed that tie. Scripture is silent about what happened to Miriam during the intervening years, but likely she suffered along with the other Israelites with the increased persecutions. Then God spoke to her brother Aaron and told him to go out into the desert and meet Moses! Surely Aaron shared this with Miriam.

Imagine her anticipation about seeing her beloved brother and the sheer joy of that reunion. Her heart must have swelled with joy and gratitude as he led the people of God out of bondage into freedom. When Moses stretched out his hand over the sea and God parted the waters, I can imagine Miriam skipping like a girl through that dry riverbed. When the wall of water collapsed over the Egyptian chariots, "the people feared the Lord and put their trust in him and in Moses his servant," and I can imagine Miriam giving Moses a high five and a two-thumbs-up YES! And she exploded in passionate praise. It began with Moses and the men singing:

> "I will sing to the Lord,
>   for he is highly exalted.
> The horse and its rider
>   he has hurled into the sea.
> The Lord is my strength and my song;
>   he has become my salvation.
> He is my God, and I will praise him,
>   my father's God, and I will exalt him."
>
> — Exodus 15:1-2

Moses continued to praise God for His mighty acts, for His love and redemption, for His power and His promise. Then Miriam

took a tambourine in her hand, and all the women followed her, with tambourines and dancing. Miriam sang to them:

> "Sing to the Lord,
>   for he is highly exalted.
> The horse and its rider
>   he has hurled into the sea."
>
> — Exodus 15:20-21

The bond between Moses and Miriam must have intensified as she supported his ministry among the people and as they joined their hearts in worship. Miriam is a model of faith and faithfulness.

She exudes the practical purity that issues forth from positional purity. But the slightest stain pollutes practical purity. God never removes His declaration of our positional purity, but when we slip into sin, we become practically soiled. Miriam slipped, and it was a painful fall.

PAINFUL PURITY

On the surface the family feud that precipitated Miriam's fall had to do with what she considered an unsuitable marriage for her brother. The biblical narrative is riveting:

> Miriam and Aaron began to talk against Moses because of his Cushite wife, for he had married a Cushite. "Has the Lord spoken only through Moses?" they asked. "Hasn't he also spoken through us?" And the Lord heard this.
>
> (Now Moses was a very humble man, more humble than anyone else on the face of the earth.)
>
> At once the Lord said to Moses, Aaron and Miriam, "Come out to the Tent of Meeting, all three of you." So the three of them came out. Then the Lord came down in a pillar of cloud; he stood at the entrance to the Tent and summoned Aaron and Miriam. When both of them stepped forward, he said, "Listen to my words:
>
> "When a prophet of the Lord is among you, I reveal myself to him in visions, I speak to him in dreams. But this is not true of my servant Moses; he is faithful in all my house. With him I speak face to face, clearly and not in riddles; he sees the form of the Lord. Why then were you not afraid to speak against my servant Moses?"
>
> The anger of the Lord burned against them, and he left them.
>
> When the cloud lifted from above the Tent, there stood Miriam—leprous, like snow. Aaron turned toward her and saw that she had leprosy, and he said to Moses, "Please, my

lord, do not hold against us the sin we have so foolishly committed. . . ."

So Moses cried out to the Lord, "O God, please heal her!"

The Lord replied to Moses, "If her father had spit in her face, would she not have been in disgrace for seven days? Confine her outside the camp for seven days; after that she can be brought back." So Miriam was confined outside the camp for seven days, and the people did not move on till she was brought back.

— Numbers 12

How could one with such unsullied purity of life slip into such humiliation? My horror is not at Miriam's actions. My horror is at how much I resonate with her actions and with the attitudes that probably prompted those actions.

Miriam's dissatisfaction had probably been brewing for some time. Perhaps she had stuffed her displeasure over an accumulation of issues. If we could listen in to her conversations with herself, perhaps we would hear things such as: "This has gone on long enough. I never bargained for months in the desert. Why doesn't Moses go ahead and take us to this promised land and let us get settled. I am tired of living out of a suitcase and being in limbo.

"There is something unfair about the organizational structure that is developing among us. Only men are being put in charge of things. Maybe that's the reason we are still stuck in this desert.

"Moses did not even notice how hard I worked to calm the women when everyone was complaining about wanting meat to eat. I spent hours listening to them and encouraging them. If it had not been for me, Moses would have had a riot on his hands. He never uttered a word of appreciation. And he even forgot my birthday!

"The women do not recognize and respect my role as prophetess. I really think Moses should require them to acknowledge my position. I should not be expected to do some of the chores they do, and maybe there should be a special title for them to use in addressing me.

"Moses has ignored my request for a better tent. After all I have done for him, I cannot believe that he has not given priority to my needs. And the elders are just as insensitive. I told them I need more space so I can minister more effectively. They don't even recognize the importance of my ministry.

"The older women have become lazy, and the younger women are arrogant. I can't depend on them, and I am left with more than my share of the responsibility. Ever since Mother left me to watch that basket, everyone has expected too much of me.

"This is surely the straw that will break my camel's back. Moses has humiliated our family by marrying that Cushite woman. I know that marrying a Cushite is not forbidden like marriage to a Canaanite, but it is beneath the spiritual position of our family. We are the first family of Israel! It's time I talk to Aaron about this. I've been thinking for a long time that Aaron and I need to assume some of the authority from Moses. We know the mind of the Lord just as well as Moses does."

I identify with Miriam. I understand exactly what she was experiencing. She was the one who stood guard over Moses' basket. As an infant, his life had been in her hands. If she had been distracted for a moment, he could have floated downstream. If she had lost her courage and failed to approach the princess and offer to find a nurse, Moses would not have had the benefit of knowing his Hebrew identity and heritage. Doesn't she deserve some credit, appreciation, and acclaim? How often I fail to heed the warning that "Pride goes before destruction, a haughty spirit before a fall" (Proverbs 16:18). Like Miriam, I fall into the bottomless pit of pride.

Pride is an abomination to the Lord. Spiritual pride is especially abominable. To take ownership of what God has done, or to take pride in the gifts of the Holy Spirit and the opportunities to use those gifts, or to misuse the gifts and opportunities is shocking and dreadful in the courts of heaven.

God intervened. Miriam was covered with the disease that screamed "unclean." The mediator cried, "O God, please heal her."

She spent seven days outside the camp. The covenant community waited until she was brought back into their fellowship.

The only other thing we read about Miriam is the account of her death and burial. At the end of the forty years of wilderness wandering, " . . . the whole Israelite community arrived at the Desert of Zin, and they stayed at Kadesh. There Miriam died and was buried" (Numbers 20:1). We can only speculate, but my hunch is that Miriam returned to her pre-pride attitude of passionate purity. In fact, I suspect she was more passionate about living a life of purity because she had experienced the painful rescue from the pit of pride. After seven days outside the camp, I suspect she also had a deeper appreciation for life in the covenant community. I also suspect that Miriam wants us to learn the horrific dangers of pride.

PRIDE AND PURITY

A prideful heart and a pure heart cannot coexist. The one crowds out the other. The virtue of purity flourishes as humility replaces pride. "The fear of the Lord teaches a man wisdom, and humility comes before honor" (Proverbs 15:33).

Humility is "the goal which God intended when he afflicted his people and toward which they are to endure affliction."[4] It expresses an absolute dependence on and submission to God. The humble desire no glory for themselves; their desire is for God to be praised.

"Miriam and Aaron divined from their own hearts, from their own proud thoughts, what the mind of the Lord might be, while Moses simply asked what the Lord had said. Moses' whole life of service was controlled by the Word of the Lord. It's so easy to become proud once we think we know something. Then we cast aside the law of the Lord and despise anyone who does not know what we think we know."[5]

The "deadly D's" of discontentment, disappointment, discouragement, and despair all thrive in a prideful heart. Even a trace of pride pollutes the heart. Pride is self-centered; humility is God-centered.

We women have a way of stuffing our displeasure until it erupts. We also have a tendency to see life in its bits and pieces rather than as a part of the flow of redemption. When we look at the individual parts of our lives, some things appear unfair and unpleasant. When we take them out of the context of the big picture, we easily drift into the attitude that we deserve better, and the tumble down into the pit of pride begins.

Pride infects the heart with leprosy. One of the first symptoms of leprosy is insensitivity to pain. The body deteriorates because the person does not feel the pain of the infections. Pride does the same thing to the heart. It desensitizes us and eats away the soul.

James asks the question:

> *What causes fights and quarrels among you? Don't they come from your desires that battle within you? You want something but don't get it. You kill and covet. . . . you quarrel and fight. . . . you ask with wrong motives, that you may spend what you get on your pleasures. You adulterous people, don't you know that friendship with the world is hatred toward God? Anyone who chooses to be a friend of the world becomes an enemy of God. Or do you think Scripture says without reason that the spirit he caused to live in us envies intensely? But he gives us more grace. That is why Scripture says: "God opposes the proud but gives grace to the humble." Submit yourselves, then, to God. Resist the devil, and he will flee from you. Come near to God and he will come near to you. Wash your hands, you sinners, and purify your hearts, you double-minded. Grieve, mourn and wail. Change your laughter to mourning and your joy to gloom. Humble yourselves before the Lord, and he will lift you up.*

> — *James 4:1-10*

Jesus said, "Blessed are the pure in heart, for they will see God" (Matthew 5:8). Positional purity that is being reflected in practical purity gives us spiritual 20/20 eyesight. We see God in all of life.

We view our world and our life with a purity of vision that acknowledges His sovereignty in every event, and the more we do this, the more we reflect His purity as we move through the bits and pieces of our life. The bits and pieces make sense as we humbly yield them to the Divine Director to use for His glorious purposes.

The more I understand this, the more fervently I pray Proverbs 3:5-6 for our grandchildren. I long for them to trust in the Lord with all their hearts and lean not on their own understanding. I pray that in all their ways they will acknowledge Him—they will bow before His sovereign rule in their lives. Then He will make their paths straight.

Shadows dim our vision. Any desire for something other than God's glory puts us under the shadow of pride. We must intentionally and decisively drive our thoughts back to the doctrine of justification. I deserve nothing but condemnation. I cannot stand in the presence of a holy God. Yet He puts the very purity of Christ over me. He looks at me and declares me to be pure because of the purity of Jesus. Tears of gratitude, wonder, and praise stain the page as I write. May the tears never cease to flow. May I never cease to thrill that my garments sparkle with the purity of Jesus.

A woman named Gloria is captivated by this truth, and her story captivated me.

PURE GLORY

The icebreaker at a women's luncheon was a clever way for us to learn and remember the names of those at our table. Each woman was to tell the story of her name. We heard some great stories, and they really did help us to remember each other's names. Then it was the turn of a woman sitting across the table from me.

"My name is Gloria," she said. "My name has a wonderful meaning, but there is a sad part to my story. My name means glory to God. Before I was born, my parents decided that if I was a girl, my dad would name me, and if I was a boy, Mom would do the honors. My dad named me, and it was not until afterwards that my mom learned that it was because he was having an affair with a woman named Gloria. When I was nine years old, it suddenly occurred to me why I had the name. My mother had never mentioned it, and she never allowed it to be a barrier between us. She loved the Lord, and she loved me unconditionally. I made a decision. I knew that I could rejoice in the meaning of my name, or I could despise the reason for my name. I could see myself as one created to glorify my heavenly Father, or I could see myself stained with the impurity of my earthly father's sin." Then with joy radiating from her face, she said, "I chose to rejoice in the meaning of my name."

We are all like Gloria. Her story is our story. Her name is our name. As Christians, we can choose to rejoice in the meaning of our life—God's glory. We can choose to dwell on the impurity of our past, or we can celebrate the purity of our position in Christ by reflecting His purity in all of life.

IN SUMMARY

The true woman is passionate about living a life of purity for the glory of her Savior. It would have been easy to write this chapter if I had discussed the obvious impurity of the new woman's lifestyle. That would have provided plenty of material to fill a chapter and would have been easy to write because those expressions of impurity are relatively easy to avoid. This chapter has been painful to write because it bores to the core of my soul. I suspect the intense spiritual battles I have fought in writing this chapter are typical of my sisters who long to express their positional purity in a life of purity. Miriam was a true woman who fought those battles. She has taught me much.

First, Miriam has taught me that the true woman can stand securely before her Father with her heart in her hand and say: "Because You have declared me pure in Your sight, I have confidence to ask You to 'Search me, O God, and know my heart; test me and know my anxious thoughts. See if there is any offensive way in me, and lead me in the way everlasting'" (Psalm 139:23-24).

Second, I have learned that when the true woman slips into sin, she has a Mediator at the right hand of the Father crying, "O God, please heal her." So we don't have to be afraid to pray, "Have mercy on me, O God, according to your unfailing love; according to your great compassion blot out my transgressions. Wash away all my iniquity and cleanse me from my sin. . . . Create in me a pure heart, O God, and renew a steadfast spirit within me" (Psalm 51:1, 2, 10).

Third, Miriam teaches us that when we sin, we must return to the covenant community. It may be painfully humiliating, but life outside the camp is not a permanent home for the true woman.

Fourth, when someone else sins, the covenant community must prayerfully wait while the person is outside the camp and then reflect God's mercy by enfolding the repentant sinner back into the fellowship.

Fifth, the true woman will passionately sing, "I delight greatly in the Lord; my soul rejoices in my God. For he has clothed me with garments of salvation and arrayed me in a robe of righteousness. . . ." (Isaiah 61:10). Then she will take the hands of her sisters and say, "Glorify the Lord with me; let us exalt his name together" (Psalm 34:3).

Personal Reflection

1. Think about your own deliverance out of sin and use the song of Moses and Miriam in Exodus 15:1-21 to write your prayer of praise to the Lord.

2. What lesson from Miriam is most applicable to you at this time in your life?

3. Memorize Proverbs 3:5-7. Write a prayer asking for wisdom to humbly acknowledge God's presence and power as you view the world and every event of your life.

UNFAITHFUL

I have always feared what would happen to me and to my family if my husband was ever unfaithful. I have had the opportunity to find out, and I know now that the love of Christ is much greater than all my fears. I also now realize my greatest fear was that I would not have the ability to truly forgive. I was right. However, the powerful work of His Spirit in me was able.

When my husband first came to me with his confession of unfaithfulness, I saw such true pain and repentance over his sin that immediate forgiveness was a very natural response. My love for him seemed, at that time, unconditional. As the days and weeks passed, and the consequences of this sin began to set heavily upon us, I knew that true forgiveness had not come so quickly.

Because my husband was a pastor, all of my life was being changed forever because of what he had done. While I was beginning to see myself more and more as a victim, God in His gracious mercy began to show me my own sin. I can hardly bear to write this down now because the pain of it all was, and is, so great. I became very angry with my husband, very angry with myself, and very angry with God. I am certain this anger would have consumed me but for two divine interventions that forced my focus on someone other than myself. I had to deal with the dying and death of my parent and the life and living of my children.

Children are indeed a blessing. When my circumstances were overwhelming, they showed me His grace. Their lives were also being disrupted, yet they were able to forgive their earthly father and trust him for their future. Could I ever again have that child-like faith and trust in my heavenly Father? With no job, no home, no church home, Jesus asked me if He could be my All Sufficient One. At this point I began to understand a few of the precious lessons He had for me.

First, I had to learn the efficacious nature of forgiveness—that is, the way that Christ forgave me. He was not a victim of my sin; He freely bore my sin. Could I bear my husband's sin as my very own? Was he not bearing much of my sin as his own each day? To bear one another's sin is to truly forgive.

Second, through this process I began to see and hate my own sin more and more. What a need I have of Christ's continual grace and mercy!

Finally, I entered into a sweeter understanding of the radical nature of repentance and forgiveness in human relationships. When there is thorough repentance and thorough forgiveness, there truly is reconciliation at the deepest level. And a reconciled relationship dramatically reflects our reconciled relationship with God.

A sweet sister who walked this road before me gave me a Scripture: "Some of the wise will stumble, so that they may be refined, purified and made spotless until the time of the end . . . " (Daniel 11:35). The refining, purifying, purging hand of almighty God is sometimes painful beyond words, yet His faithfulness is also beyond words. Through my deepest fears, I have been kept close by the strong arms of my loving Father, and I have seen Him make my precious husband into a man after His own heart. His Word is true.

—Name withheld

$\mathcal{D}$OMESTICITY

*Whatever breaks down the modest reserve, the domestic
virtues, the persuasive gentleness, of woman, is an
injury done to the community.*

Female Piety

This chapter is an affirmation and celebration of home. I
promise I am not going to say that you must rush out and buy
Martha Stewart's latest video and learn to grow bug-free roses,
match your plaids and florals, prepare gourmet lunches, and sten-
cil the lunch bags. Neither am I going to back away from acknowl-
edging domesticity as a virtue Christian women should cultivate.
However, I do admit that I approach this topic with considerable
trepidation. Let me explain my hesitancy.

As I write and speak about biblical womanhood, I get letters.
Most of them are encouraging testimonies that thrill my heart, but
some make me sad because some women hear me say things I am
not saying. I appreciate these letters, as they remind me how careful we must be in communicating clearly. But I realize that no matter how clearly we communicate, some women have mental
gridlock—they are bound to their own situations.

Our own situation often restrains our ability to hear everything that is said. We *interpret what we hear* in light of our situation
rather than *apply what we hear* to our situation. We lock into what

we think we hear, particularly when it is an emotional issue. Domesticity is an emotional issue. I think the reason is that when we hear the word, we assume specific behaviors. If those behaviors don't fit our situation, we feel that others are making unfair judgments. Carol and Lisa illustrate how this can happen.

Carol's husband left her and their three children. The child support she received barely covered the house payment. As this painful situation unfolded, Carol faced the reality that she could no longer be a stay-at-home mom. We talked about her fears of returning to the business world, and we spent much time working through the adjustments she and her children had to make.

At the same time, Carol's friend Lisa was expecting her first baby. Lisa and her husband made the decision that Lisa would stop working. My conversations with Lisa enthusiastically supported her decision and helped her work through the realities, fears, and adjustments of becoming a one-income family. Sometimes I talked to these two young women together. Both of them were making prayerful, wise decisions, but their decisions demanded different behaviors. If Carol had only heard what I said to Lisa, she could have interpreted it to mean that it was wrong for her to work outside the home. If Lisa had only heard what I said to Carol, she could have assumed that she had a responsibility to provide financial support for her family. Both Carol and Lisa were expressing the virtue of domesticity, though their situations demanded different actions.

The bottom line—don't limit domesticity to stay-at-home women who bake their own bread. Let's discover a biblical perspective of this concept that is applicable to women in all situations and life stages.

I believe this virtue applies to the single woman as well as to the married woman. I will use two biblical examples in this chapter. One was definitely a single woman, and there is no mention of the other's marital status. Lynn Brookside's testimony in chapter 5 tells how the admonitions to wives and mothers about the family should be applied by the single woman to her relationships in the family of God.

DOMESTICITY DEFINED

Domesticity means a devotion to home life. It pertains to the family or household. The strongest, most definitive statement on domesticity was made by Jesus: "Do not let your hearts be troubled. . . . In my Father's house are many rooms. . . . I am going there to prepare a place for you" (John 14:1-2).

The virtue of domesticity begins with an untroubled heart that has been redeemed from sin and is focused on our heavenly home. This virtue is expressed as we prepare places on earth that depict our heavenly home. This is accomplished as we reflect the character of Jesus in our homes and churches, thus making them homey places where troubled hearts find rest and safety. So domestic deeds are rooted in our theology.

Woman's helper design draws us to the domestic mission of cultivating community. The psalmist says that "our daughters will be like pillars, carved to adorn a palace" (Psalm 144:12). The Hebrew word for pillar that is used here means a corner connecting pillar. This expresses woman's capacity to beautifully connect people together in community or family.

This definition of domesticity is seen in the proverb: "The wise woman builds her house, but with her own hands the foolish one tears hers down" (Proverbs 14:1). This is obviously not the physical structure. It is the building of loving, caring relationships in the home and church. This virtue is tied to wisdom—that way of thinking about and reacting to life's experiences that reflects the teaching of a personal God who is holy, righteous, and just and who expects those living in covenant relationship with Him to reflect His character in the practical affairs of life.

The following quotes from the nineteenth-century preacher John Angell James underscore the high priority the Puritans put on family and on the woman's role in the family.

. . . home, sweet home, is the sphere of wedded woman's mission . . . to make one such home a seat of holiness and happiness; to fill one such sphere with an influence so sweet and sacred; to throw the fascination of connubial feeling and of maternal influence over one such community; to irradiate so many countenances with delight; to fill so many hearts with content, and to prepare so many characters for their future part in life; such an object would be deemed by an angel worth an incarnation upon earth.

. . . the springs of an empire's prosperity lie in the domestic constitution, and in well-trained families. . . . Even one such family is a contribution to the majestic flow of a nation's greatness. Can such families exist without a woman's care, and oversight, and wisdom? Has it not grown into a proverb, that home has ever been the nursery of great men, and their mothers their instructresses? It may be said as a general principle, that woman is not only the mother of the body, but of the character, of her children. To her is first entrusted the instruction of the mind, the cultivation of the heart, the formation of the life. Thought, feeling, will, imagination, virtue, religion, or the contrary moral tendencies, all germinate under her fostering influence. "The greatest power in the moral world is that which a mother exercises over her young child." The decisive moment in education is the starting point. The dominant direction which is to determine the whole course of life, lies concealed in the first years of infancy; and these belong to the mother.[1]

I very distinctly perceive, and as impressively feel, the importance of the female character on account of its influence upon the well-being of society. And it is clear to me, that woman's is a domestic mission, which is to affect society through the medium of family influence. As she fills up her place with wisdom and propriety, so will she promote the well-being of the community. Nor is it society only, but the Church of Christ, that is concerned in, and promoted by, the female character.[2]

Even Christian women often cringe at such notions because we live in a culture that degrades domestic virtues. George Grant has written that Betty Friedan's *The Feminine Mystique*

> warned that among other things depression, addiction, and even suicide stalk women who spend too much time in their home harboring Victorian ideals. Perhaps feeling that she wasn't quite making herself clear on the issue, she went on to argue that none but the mentally retarded could find housework fulfilling, and that women who accept the role of housewife are in as much danger as the millions who walked to their own deaths in Nazi gas chambers. In the days that followed, Friedan's rhetoric contributed mightily to the editorial profile of virtually all of the women's magazines. . . . Each gleefully trampled upon everything associated with domesticity with the pious assurance that such things were not merely beneath the dignity of women, they were downright menacing.

> But then in 1987 Nancy Lindemeyer, Cindy Sperling, Susan Maher—all veterans of the traditional feminist publishing industry—decided to launch a revolution. They decided to reinvent the women's magazine.

> At first glance, the product of their labors, *Victoria*, doesn't look terribly serious, much less revolutionary. A serious women's magazine, according to the tenets of feminist orthodoxy, covers politics, economics, science, business, and other worldly affairs. *Victoria* by contrast is resolutely domestic. . . .

> This brash reinvention of the women's magazine reinvests the home with mind and character and rehabilitates the lost arts of hearth and home.

> It has been able to do all this because its effort was rooted first and foremost in a worldview shift. As publisher Cindy Sperling has said, "We profile a kind of post-feminist worldview, not just a pre-feminist worldview." Either way, though, it rejects the dominant feminist worldview.

And that is a dramatic departure. . . . though it falls far short of an authentically biblical vision, it certainly does highlight the innate hunger for domesticity that even the most thoroughly modern American woman yearns for.

Grant concludes by saying that the demise of feminism does none of us "any substantive good if the only ones to take advantage of the situation are secular publishers. Moments like these call for more than Victoria's Secret; they call for Christ's Evangel."[3]

Proverbs 31 gives us the substantive significance of domesticity because it gives us Christ's Evangel.

DOMESTICITY DESCRIBED

The Proverbs 31 sketch of a noble woman says a lot about her domestic deeds. One verse is especially intriguing: "When it snows, she has no fear for her household; for all of them are clothed in scarlet" (Proverbs 31:21).

There must be more to this verse than what is on the surface. I realize the importance of good planning, careful budgeting, and other skills required to care for a family, but surely there is more involved than dialing Land's End and ordering red wool sweaters for my family. As I probed this proverb, I gleaned a perspective about domesticity that I think is valid. It started with scrutinizing the key words.

Snow is used in two ways in Scripture. It is used in reference to judgment, with leprosy described as being white as snow (Exodus 4:6; Numbers 12:10; 2 Kings 5:27). It is also used in reference to cleansing: "Cleanse me with hyssop, and I will be clean; wash me, and I will be whiter than snow" (Psalm 51:7).

Scarlet is associated with luxury (2 Samuel 1:24). Scarlet material was used in the tabernacle (Exodus 26:1, 31; 28:5-8, 33). It is also mentioned in purification ceremonies where it symbolized blood (Leviticus 14:4, 6, 49, 52). We see this symbolism in Matthew 27:28: "They stripped him and put a scarlet robe on him. . . . "

Both of these words are seen in Isaiah 1:18:

"Come now, let us reason together," says the Lord. "Though your sins are like scarlet, they shall be as white as snow; though they are red as crimson, they shall be like wool."

Clothed is used in reference to our salvation: "For he has clothed me with garments of salvation and arrayed me in a robe of righteousness . . . " (Isaiah 61:10). Paul wrote to the Galatians: "You are all sons of God through faith in Christ Jesus, for all of you who were baptized into Christ have clothed yourselves with Christ" (Galatians 3:26-27).

In these passages we see that we are under judgment, but God makes provision for our cleansing through the blood of Christ. He then clothes us with the luxurious, pristine righteousness of Christ.

So perhaps domesticity goes beyond the provision for warm clothes during bad weather. It includes that kind of caring, but it is more. The woman with this virtue does not fear the judgment for her family because they have been cleansed and clothed by the blood of the Savior. Rahab illustrates this.

RADICAL RAHAB

Rahab is an unlikely candidate for Queen of Domesticity. She was an unmarried Canaanite harlot.

When Joshua sent the spies to Jericho, "they entered the house of a prostitute named Rahab" (Joshua 2:1). The king of Jericho sent a message to Rahab to hand the men over, but she hid them and sent the soldiers on a wild goose chase.

One wonders if Rahab had previous experience hiding her "guests" and convincing those looking for them that they were gone. But this time was different because Rahab's motive was different. God's grace preceded the spies, and His providence guided them to the woman He had chosen to redeem.

We don't know how Rahab heard about the God of Israel.

Perhaps travelers frequented her place of business and told about the exploits of the Israelites. Perhaps she had been hearing about these people wandering in the wilderness for years. But at this point in time God's grace applied that knowledge in a decisive and positive way, and Rahab said:

> *"I know that the Lord has given this land to you and that a great fear of you has fallen on us, so that all who live in this country are melting in fear because of you. We have heard how the Lord dried up the water of the Red Sea for you when you came out of Egypt, and what you did to Sihon and Og, the two kings of the Amorites east of the Jordan, whom you completely destroyed. When we heard of it, our hearts melted and everyone's courage failed because of you, for the Lord your God is God in heaven above and on the earth below. Now then, please swear to me by the Lord that you will show kindness to my family, because I have shown kindness to you. Give me a sure sign that you will spare the lives of my father and mother, my brothers and sisters, and all who belong to them, and that you will save us from death."*
>
> — *Joshua 2:8-13*

Rahab took a radical risk. Hiding the spies was not the most expedient thing to do. If the king of Jericho discovered her plot, he would have her killed. Here is a crisis of faith. Where would Rahab put her hope for salvation from the coming judgment? What Rahab did was radical, but it was not a risk. The risk factor dissipated when Rahab's knowledge of God moved from an intellectual assent to information about Him to ultimate trust in Him. Rahab called Him Lord. This is His personal name of covenant faithfulness by which He bound Himself to Israel. She acknowledged Him as the sovereign God of heaven and earth. She asked for kindness. This is the Hebrew word *chesed*, which often refers to God's mercy in accordance with His promises.

God was merciful. He brought Rahab home to Himself and

gave her a love for home. The first fruit of her faith was a concern for her family. This, too, is radical.

Considering Rahab's profession, it is likely that she was estranged from her family. They were probably embarrassed by her and perhaps even had disowned her. Yet her foremost considera-tion was their safety. "The wise woman builds her house, but with her own hands the foolish one tears hers down" (Proverbs 14:1).

The men agreed to spare Rahab and her family on two condi-tions. She must tie a scarlet cord in her window, and all of her fam-ily must be in her house.

When the Israelites crossed the Jordan River and began their march around Jericho, the citizenry must have been terrified—all except Rahab. She was not afraid of the judgment because her fam-ily was covered in scarlet. Scarlet is the symbol of redemption. Stop and ponder this graphic illustration of our redemption.

When the walls of Jericho collapsed, "the young men who had done the spying went in and brought out Rahab, her father and mother and brothers and all who belonged to her. They brought out her entire family . . . " (Joshua 6:23).

One wonders what it took to persuade her entire family to come to her house. My mind goes wild imagining the reconcilia-tions that would have been necessary. There must have been a rad-ical change in Rahab for them to believe her warning and to agree to enter her house as the neighbors watched and whispered.

God did not ignore or approve of Rahab's sin. His grace redeemed her from it. Rahab's faith and obedience are commended in the New Testament (Hebrews 11:31 and James 2:25). Even more astounding, God actually incorporated Rahab into the family tree of His Son. Rahab married Salmon and became the mother of Boaz. Boaz married another outsider, the Moabitess Ruth. Ruth's son Obed was the father of Jesse, the father of David.

And it all began when God's long arm of salvation reached into the house of a harlot and she made the radical decision to trust Him. Her family came into her house, and they were saved from the judgment, and through her family the Savior came into the world to save His people from the judgment. From Rahab we can learn important principles about clothing our families with scarlet.

First, we must cast ourselves on the mercy of the Lord God. He is God in heaven above and on the earth below. This earth will go the way of Jericho. Our only hope for deliverance is to be covered with the blood of Jesus.

Second, we must live an example of radical faith before our families. Rahab defied her culture and lived by faith regardless of the apparent consequences because she understood the eternal consequences. Radical obedience gives substantive proof to our families that our faith matters.

Third, we must understand and embrace God's covenant promises and commands to families:

I will establish my covenant as an everlasting covenant between me and you and your descendants after you for the generations to come, to be your God and the God of your descendants after you.

— Genesis 17:7

The children of your servants will live in your presence; their descendants will be established before you.

— Psalm 102:28

He decreed statutes for Jacob and established the law in Israel, which he commanded our forefathers to teach their children, so the next generation would know them, even the children yet to be born, and they in turn would tell their children. Then they would put their trust in God and would not forget his deeds but would keep his commands.

— Psalm 78:5-7

Fourth, we must identify ourselves with the people of God. This means moving beyond a casual involvement in our local church. Rahab did not retain her citizenship in Jericho. Her attachment and devotion to the people of God was radical. Israel became her home. Mothers, grandmothers, aunts, and friends who take children to church and enfold them into the life of the covenant community help them to make this identification. These women make church feel like home for God's people.

Fifth, it is never too late, and we are never too far away to be touched by grace. The same is true for family members who are living in sin in Jericho. They may resist our faith and our faithfulness and call us radical, but we must not compromise. We must pray.

Rahab did not fit the mold. Maybe our Father is warning us not to have a mold and insist that all women fit into it. Rahab was not a likely choice for Queen of Domesticity, but because of God's grace, her life is a radical statement of this virtue and a substantive statement of Christ's Evangel.

DEVOTED DORCAS

In Acts we read of a more traditional expression of domesticity. "In Joppa there was a disciple named Tabitha (which, when translated, is Dorcas), who was always doing good and helping the poor" (Acts 9:36).

Rahab splashed across the pages of Scripture, but Dorcas tiptoed in and out almost unnoticed—until God miraculously raised her from the dead!

Dorcas died, and there was such distress among the church in Joppa that they sent for Peter. When Peter arrived at the house where the body of Dorcas had been taken, the grieving widows showed him the clothes she had made for them. "Peter sent them all out of the room; then he got down on his knees and prayed. Turning toward the dead woman, he said, 'Tabitha, get up.' She opened her eyes, and seeing Peter she sat up. He took her by the hand and helped her to her feet. Then he called the believers and the widows and presented her to them alive. This became known all over Joppa, and many people believed in the Lord" (Acts 9:40-42).

I am fascinated by this story. Dorcas is one of my all-time

favorite women in the church. Why did her death cause such sorrow in the Joppa church family that they sent for Peter? Surely she was not the first member of their congregation to die. Why did God choose to raise her from the dead? If He was going to raise her, why did He allow her to die?

Consider the context of this event. "Then the church throughout Judea, Galilee and Samaria enjoyed a time of peace. It was strengthened and encouraged by the Holy Spirit; it grew in numbers, living in the fear of the Lord" (Acts 9:31). Then we read that Peter traveled about the country, and Scripture tells us things he did to encourage the church. A paralytic was healed in Lydda, Dorcas was raised from the dead in Joppa, and a centurion was converted in Caesarea.

God strengthened and encouraged the church in Joppa by removing a member and then giving that member back to them. Raising anyone from the dead would have been spectacular, but it was especially encouraging because it was a beloved member of this household of faith. It is encouraging to me because it was a woman. It was not a woman with a highly visible ministry. It was a woman who quietly went about taking meals to the sick, helping the poor, and making clothes for the widows. It was a wise woman who built the Lord's house by making it feel like home for His people.

Dorcas's brand of domesticity demands stamina, discipline, sensitivity, and love. Dorcas was a devoted doer. When she was removed from that church family, men and women felt a huge hole in their midst.

We must not reverse the order of what we learn about this woman. First, she was a disciple. Second, she did good works. Her deeds of domesticity expressed her relationship as a disciple of Jesus. As a disciple, Dorcas was devoted to creating a sense of family in her church, because she was devoted to the people in her church. Dorcas loved Jesus, and she loved His people. His people were her people. She devoted herself to caring for them in ordinary ways—how extraordinary!

DOMESTICITY DEFENDED

This chapter is not about being Susie Homemaker, but neither is it intended to belittle homemaking skills. Creating the ambiance of a loving home and church is a woman's prerogative and privilege.

A friend of mine was discipling a young woman who was a major messy. They had worked on cultivating the disciplines of Bible study, prayer, and Scripture memorization. Then one day my friend said, "Now we have to do something about your house."

The young woman was surprised. "It doesn't matter. My husband is just as messy as I am. Neither of us would be happy without our clutter, and the kids would probably think they were in the wrong house."

My friend persisted. On Sunday the young husband talked with my friend and assured her that he was quite happy and really preferred things as they were. My friend still persisted. "This is an aspect of your discipleship." Then my friend marshaled the troops to help the young woman. One woman in the church who had organizational skills spent a day helping her organize her cabinets and closets. Another taught her how to plan meals and shop with a list, and another taught her how to clean and how to delegate chores to her children. Then a woman helped her decorate her home. The transformation was remarkable.

Several weeks later the young husband again approached my friend. "I didn't think it mattered, but it does. I can hardly wait to get home now. Home has become a haven from the chaos of the world. The amazing thing is that I feel closer to my wife and appreciate her more than I could have imagined."

The Puritan perspective of family life verifies the validity of my friend's insistence that the young woman learn domestic skills. J. I. Packer writes:

> Puritan teachers thought humane family life, in which Christian love and joy would find full and free expression, could not be achieved till the ordered pattern they envis-

aged—the regular authority-structure and daily routine—had been firmly established. Their passion to please God expressed itself in an ardor for order; their vision of the good and godly life was of a planned, well-thought-out flow of activities in which all obligations were recognized and met, and time was found for everything that mattered: for personal devotion, for family worship, for household tasks, for wage-earning employment, for intimacy with spouse and children, for Sabbath rest, and whatever else one's calling or callings required.[4]

IN SUMMARY

My thirteen-year-old friend Jessica Jakes is a true woman with a heavenly perspective of home. Jessica and her family made several moves in a short span of time. A sympathetic adult was talking with her about how disorienting it must be to have moved so much. "When you think of home, what place do you think about?" he asked. Without missing a beat Jessica replied, "Heaven."

When a woman is gripped by this perspective, she will sacrificially care for her own family and the family of God. She will do all she can to put them under the protective, cleansing blood of Jesus. Then she will make home a place where family loves to gather, where troubled hearts find safety. She will make home a place that reflects her heavenly home. "Through wisdom a house is built, and through understanding it is established; through knowledge its rooms are filled with rare and beautiful treasures" (Proverbs 24:3-4). I don't think this means material riches; it is the knowledge of Jesus wisely worked out in practical, pleasant family life.

The true woman does not compartmentalize domesticity, nor does she reduce it to a set of behaviors. Yet she does not minimize domestic tasks because she sees them as a sacred trust.

The lessons from Rahab and Dorcas may look different, but they are the same message. They blend together to give a balanced, substantive view of domesticity. When we radically embrace the Gospel, we will be devoted to caring for God's people. For the wife and mother, this begins at home. For all of us, it includes the church. When home and church are safe, homey places, this domestic influence is felt in society.

As with every virtue, the reference point for domesticity is our relationship to God. John Angell James reminds us of this:

> You may have been the most exalted, noble, and learned of women; the most faithful of wives; the most devoted of mothers; and the kindest of mistresses; but if, with all this, you have not had repentance toward God, faith in our Lord Jesus, and true holiness, your domestic virtues, as they had in themselves no relation, and in their performance no reference, to God, will, in the end, meet with no recompense from him, and instead of "Well done, good and faithful servant," you will hear nothing more than, "They had their reward."[5]

Personal Reflection

1. Read John 14:1-3 and write a prayer thanking God for your heavenly home.

2. Is your heart troubled? View whatever is troubling your heart from the perspective that Jesus has prepared a safe place for you.

3. Are there members of your family who are not "covered in scarlet"? Make a list and begin praying regularly for their salvation.

4. Write a biblical apologetic (explanation) for celebrating your domestic tasks.

5. If you need help in making your home a homey and ordered place, ask someone to help you.

6. Get together with other women from your church and discuss the following:

Is our church a homey place?

What can we do to make it more like home?

Do younger women in our church need older women to train them in domestic deeds? How can we facilitate this?

$\mathcal{R}$EDEEMING
YOUR MARRIAGE

"Let the redeemed of the Lord say so, whom he hath redeemed from the hand of the enemy" (Psalm 107:2 KJV). The Lord redeemed my marriage from the hand of the enemy, and I want to say so.

My marriage went from technicolor to black and white. I was trusting Christ for salvation, working hard in the church, loving being a mother, teaching Bible studies, having wonderful fellowship with my Christian friends, but I was in the hands of the enemy. I secretly resented my role as a wife and my responsibility to be loving, affectionate, helpful, and encouraging to my husband.

Before marriage I was attracted to my husband's strong personality. After marriage this same personality overwhelmed me. I began believing the lie that Eve believed in the Garden—I could not be fulfilled doing it God's way. I believed the lies that I would have to fight for my rights and that it was my responsibility to destroy my husband's ego, so I did everything I could to belittle him. I corrected him in public. I rarely expressed admiration or appreciation. In trying to destroy his pride, I was destroying his manhood and elevating my own pride.

I convinced myself that when he changed, I would be a great wife. I was less and less interested in him. There were no feelings of affection or love. I would rather have gone to an execution than to bed with my husband. I turned off all the music and wore flannel nightgowns. I resented the fact that my husband was so needy, ignoring the truth that perfect Adam also had needs.

I was no longer in love with my husband because I stopped focusing on the reason I had married him. I went through the motions of being a wife. I fooled everyone except myself and God. I was miserable, and I expected to live the rest of my days enduring my role of being the wife of this man.

But Paul's words to the Ephesians can be applied to my marriage: "But because of his great love for us, God, who is rich in mercy, made us alive with Christ even when we were dead in transgressions—it is by grace you have been saved" (Ephesians 2:4-5).

God made me aware of my rebellion. He showed me that I could go through the motions of being spiritual, but that I could not have a right relationship with Him if my relationship with my husband was disobedient, strained, and selfish. He brought me to the place where I was willing for Him to work on my marriage, but I did not really believe that He could do anything about the desire of my heart. I was so wrong.

It began with the painful conviction that I was emasculating my husband and that I could not think of myself as a spiritual woman if I was not being the kind of wife God created me to be. The Holy Spirit gave me repenting grace, changed my attitude, softened my heart, and slowly convinced me that God could and would redeem my marriage. He enabled me to make a renewed commitment to Christ, to His Word, and to the vow that I took the day I was married. I rolled up my sleeves and went to work cleaning up the mess of my marriage. This was my task, my ministry, my calling.

From Titus 2 I came to understand that I had to learn to love my husband. I learned that this is a love of commitment, of knowledge, of the will, and a desire to obey God.

I applied Scriptures to my marriage that I had previously applied to other relationships.

Do nothing out of selfish ambition or vain conceit, but in humility consider others better than yourselves. Each of you should look not only to your own interests, but also to the interests of others.

— *Philippians 2:3-4*

Accept one another, then, just as Christ accepted you, in order to bring praise to God.

— *Romans 15:7*

It is to a man's honor to avoid strife, but every fool is quick to quarrel.

— *Proverbs 20:3*

Do not say, "I'll pay you back for this wrong!" Wait for the Lord, and he will deliver you.

— *Proverbs 20:22*

I began to really believe that Jesus was by my side in my marriage. Sometimes I would say in my heart, "Jesus, he's acting like a jerk. I am angry and resentful. Help me." There was peace rather than rage. And love grew. It did not happen overnight. It took time, patience, work, and many failures.

As I gradually accepted my husband's need for me to be his helper and that God had designed me for that task, I began to understand my ministry in our marriage. I began to understand that I am God's gift to my husband. I was created for this, but I also volunteered for it when I stood at the altar. As I began submitting to his need for me to be his helper rather than trying to change him, I began to see wonderful changes. He became less proud and more sensitive. I look for opportunities to forgive, to be kind and gracious, to do for him what I do for people at church. I stopped expecting my husband to meet needs only Christ can meet. I started building my husband up rather than tearing him down.

Love grew, and it continues to grow. God changed my heart, my emotions, my desires, and my husband! I can honestly say I love my husband more today than I did when I married him.

Satan went to Eve in the Garden to destroy that home; he came to me with the same lies to destroy my home. But God visited that Garden and gave the promise of redemption. God visited my home and kept that promise.

There is no relationship on earth that God cannot redeem. With Him, there are no irreconcilable differences.

—Name withheld

𝒮UBMISSION

*My object has been to promote the happiness of both
sexes, by improving the character of the one on which so
much of the happiness of both depends; and to advance
the welfare of society by purifying its earthly source.*

Female Piety

I f the defining virtues of the true woman are provocative, this
particular virtue out-provokes the others. The new woman cannot bear the sound of this word. Yet without trying to be con-
tentious, I am declaring my allegiance to this virtue by stating
unequivocally that this is the defining virtue of the defining
virtues. This is where the rubber meets the road. This is the water-
shed issue for the true woman. Submission goes to the center of
our heart; it is the infrastructure of our obedience. There is probably nothing that exposes our hearts as plainly and painfully as our
attitude about submission.

As I have said elsewhere:

Headship and submission are two sides of one coin. They
go together. But neither is exempt if the other forfeits.

Headship and submission begin with a spirit of humility:
"God opposes the proud but gives grace to the humble.
Submit yourselves, then, to God." (James 4:6-7)

Humility then expresses itself in mutual submission: "Submit to one another out of reverence for Christ." (Ephesians 5:21)

Humility continues to express itself in headship and submission.

Submission, whether it is to God, to one another, to husbands, or to male leadership in the Church, is a grace-empowered virtue of humility and reverence for God. It has nothing to do with superior/inferior status or equality. It has to do with attitude and function. The Father, Son, and Holy Spirit are equal in being and in power, but each has a different function.[1]

Submission is not about behaviors; it is about character.

Let me begin with some points of clarification, though I will not elaborate on these because this chapter is not a doctrinal exposition on submission. It is a practical application of a doctrinal position. The following simply states what I believe is a biblical position. It is this position upon which this chapter is crafted.

First, every woman is not to submit to every man, but every married woman is to submit to her husband. The scriptural command to women is that we are to "be submissive to your husbands" (1 Peter 3:1). In Titus 2 we read that older women are to teach younger women to "be subject to their husbands."

Second, women are not to submit to sin. Sometimes it is very clear when that line has been crossed. Sometimes the line, or the vision of the line, is blurred. When the authority of the husband cannot be trusted, I encourage a woman to seek the advice, authority, and protection of the elders of her church.

Third, the biblical commands about women not usurping authority have reference to the home and church, not society in general.

Fourth, all believers, men and women, are to submit to the ordained leadership of the church.

Fifth, as members of the body of Christ, we are to submit to one another, regardless of gender. This is a pivotal issue for the covenant community.

As with the other virtues of the true woman, I believe this has application for the single woman and the married woman. Single women should know the biblical teaching about submission so they can encourage their married friends to obey this command, so they will understand the concept if they ever consider marriage, and because they are called to submit to the authority of the elders of their church. The biblical example I use in this chapter is a married woman, and her behaviors are in the context of marriage, but the salient message is about her character.

We will look at this virtue through the example of Rebekah. My prayer is that it will be a caution, a challenge, and a celebration.

THE YOUNG WOMAN

The woman of noble character who fears the Lord is described as one who "opens her arms to the poor and extends her hands to the needy" (Proverbs 31:20).

I wonder if Abraham's servant was thinking about this when he prayed:

> "O Lord, God of my master Abraham, give me success today, and show kindness to my master Abraham. See, I am standing beside this spring, and the daughters of the townspeople are coming out to draw water. May it be that when I say to a girl, 'Please let down your jar that I may have a drink,' and she says, 'Drink, and I'll water your camels too,'—let her be the one you have chosen for your servant Isaac. By this I will know that you have shown kindness to my master."
>
> — Genesis 24:12-14

This trusted servant was on a mission to get a wife for Abraham's son Isaac. Abraham made it clear that this was no ordinary marriage arrangement. This involved the covenant promise.

"The Lord, the God of heaven, who brought me out of my father's household and my native land and who spoke to me and promised me on oath, saying 'To your offspring I will give this land'—he will send his angel before you so that you can get a wife for my son ..."

— *Genesis 24:7*

This chief servant in Abraham's household was in charge of everything Abraham had, but he had never been given such a formidable responsibility. What would he look for? Would he find the most beautiful girl, or the brightest, or the most successful? Would he look for the one who made the best fashion statement? As questions swirled in his mind, perhaps he remembered Abraham's beloved wife, Sarah. Perhaps this wise servant knew that it was not Sarah's beauty that bound Abraham's heart to her; it was her character. Sarah ... the one about whom it would be written hundreds of years later:

Wives, in the same way be submissive to your husbands so that, if any of them do not believe the word, they may be won over without words by the behavior of their wives, when they see the purity and reverence of your lives. Your beauty should not come from outward adornment, such as braided hair and the wearing of gold jewelry and fine clothes. Instead, it should be that of your inner self, the unfading beauty of a gentle and quiet spirit, which is of great worth in God's sight. For this is the way the holy women of the past who put their hope in God used to make themselves beautiful. They were submissive to their own husbands, like Sarah, who obeyed Abraham and called him her master. You are her daughters if you do what is right and do not give way to fear.

— *1 Peter 3:1-6*

Now the servant knew what he was looking for, but he still had a question. How would he know which girl had a pure, reverent, gentle, quiet, submissive spirit? Why of course . . . the one who opened her arms to the poor and extended her hands to the needy— to the weary traveler and his stinking camels. So he prayed.

"Before he had finished praying, Rebekah came out with her jar on her shoulder. She was the daughter of Bethuel son of Milcah, who was the wife of Abraham's brother Nahor. The girl was very beautiful, a virgin; no man had ever lain with her. She went down to the spring, filled her jar and came up again."

Could this be the one? The servant's heart pounded as he hurried to meet her. His voice trembled as he said, "Please give me a little water from your jar."

"Drink, my lord," she said and quickly lowered the jar to her hands and gave him a drink.

The servant could barely swallow. The silence seemed endless, and then she said, "I'll draw water for your camels too, until they have finished drinking."

Bingo! She must be the one. She had no reason to be so kind except that it was an expression of her character. She did not know who this man was. She had no agenda. When she finished watering the camels, he asked, "Whose daughter are you?"

"I am the daughter of Bethuel, the son that Milcah bore to Nahor."

"Then the man bowed down and worshipped the Lord, saying, 'Praise be to the Lord, the God of my master Abraham, who has not abandoned his kindness and faithfulness to my master. As for me, the Lord has led me on the journey to the house of my master's relatives'" (Genesis 24: 15-27).

The servant went home with Rebekah, told her father and brother about his mission, and they agreed that Rebekah should return with him and become Isaac's wife. But they hesitated. "Let the girl remain with us ten days or so; then you may go." The servant persisted, so they said, "Let's call the girl and ask her about it."

This is one of Rebekah's finest moments. When they asked, "Will you go with this man?" she did not flinch. "I will go."

This was not a young woman with an adventuresome spirit.

Rebekah knew this was a costly decision and that it was for keeps. I believe this was an act of faith in the covenant promise and in the God who made the promise. This was an expression of a character that was being shaped and driven by God's Word and His Spirit. This was a true woman.

THE BRIDE

The tender romance of the biblical account is charming.

> *Now Isaac . . . went out to the field one evening to meditate, and as he looked up, he saw camels approaching. Rebekah also looked up and saw Isaac. She got down from her camel and asked the servant, "Who is that man in the field coming to meet us?"*
>
> *"He is my master," the servant answered. So she took her veil and covered herself.*
>
> *Then the servant told Isaac all he had done. Isaac brought her into the tent of his mother Sarah, and he married Rebekah. So she became his wife, and he loved her; and Isaac was comforted after his mother's death.*
>
> — Genesis 24:62-67

Rebekah brought community and compassion into Isaac's tent, and he was comforted. Neither her beauty nor her intellect could have comforted him; her character won his heart. Isaac's tent became a place of passionate romance and pensive reflection, of seriousness and silliness, of commemorating the past and daydreaming about the future. Rebekah carefully cultivated her relationship with her husband, and she was a channel of compassion to him. Isaac was comforted. His tent was a good place to be. His troubled heart found safety there.

Isaac flourished. He became what every Christian woman longs for in a husband. He was a man who was sensitive to his wife's needs, and he prayed for her. "Isaac prayed to the Lord on behalf of his wife, because she was barren."

Rebekah also flourished. When she became pregnant with twins, and the babies "jostled each other within her," she inquired of the Lord. He gave her a glimpse of His plan:

> "Two nations are in your womb, and two peoples from within you will be separated; one people will be stronger than the other, and the older will serve the younger."
>
> — Genesis 25:23

There was domestic tranquillity in this home. Rebekah comforted Isaac; he became a spiritual leader in his tent; she grew spiritually and gained a deeper understanding of the covenant promise. The two became one (Genesis 2:24). This is Christian marriage as it should be.

A man and a woman who individually live in God's presence are able to live in one another's presence in a profound way. They can reflect God's character to one another. They reflect their covenant relationship with God in their relationship with one another. Their oneness with God empowers them to overcome self-centeredness, thus making oneness with each other a possibility. When there is a growing, deepening oneness, submission is almost a nonissue, because these marriage partners seldom have to consciously think about it. Oneness eliminates the separateness that makes submission oppressive.

In her novel based on the family of Jonathan and Sarah Edwards, Edna Gerstner wrote:

> [Sarah Edwards] unconsciously exerted her charm on all she met. She always stirred in the opposite sex admiration and an awareness of her femininity. She had that quality of making a man awake to the fact that she was different, a creature of gossamer substance against which his own masculinity became more apparent, and which caused him to lift his

shoulders and even to strut a little. . . . Even her own son was not immune to this femininity of his mother. He never forgot when he rode with her that she was a woman and that he was her protector. He became a little man. She brought out every quality of manhood in him. And even while her eyes were alert to the dangers of the forest she indulged and encouraged this strength in him and let him feel it was he upon whom their safety rested. It was good, she felt, for Jonathan to strut a little.[2]

I suspect that Isaac strutted in and out of his tent.

Now fast-forward a couple of decades. Rather than finding a blissful bride, we encounter a bitter woman.

THE WOMAN

The story is agonizingly familiar. Isaac is old, weak, and almost blind. He calls for his firstborn twin, Esau, tells him to go hunt some wild game, prepare it for him to eat, and then receive the blessing.

Rebekah was eavesdropping. She quickly called the second-born twin, Jacob, and gave him instructions: "Go out to the flock and bring me two choice young goats, so I can prepare some tasty food for your father, just the way he likes it. Then take it to your father to eat, so that he may give you his blessing before he dies."

Jacob said, "But my brother Esau is a hairy man, and I'm a man with smooth skin. What if my father touches me?" (Genesis 27:11-12).

No problem—Rebekah had an agenda and a strategy. She covered Jacob's hands and neck with the goatskins and deceived her husband.

The guileless girl became a conniving woman. The beauty became a beast. The girl who opened her arms and extended her hands to the stranger and his camels closes her fist and defiantly disobeys the authority of her husband. Submission has become an issue. A true woman became a new woman.

What happened?

We must get into Rebekah's sandals and learn from her, for the same thing can happen to any of us. If we look closely, I think we can find some caution signals. I think, too, that Rebekah would want us to learn from her life. The lessons are too valuable to waste.

Caution Signal #1

The boys grew up, and Esau became a skillful hunter, a man of the open country, while Jacob was a quiet man, staying among the tents. Isaac, who had a taste for wild game, loved Esau, but Rebekah loved Jacob.

— Genesis 25:27-28

This family system is in trouble. There is division between the parents and competition between the brothers. Sadly, this is often the case when children are allowed to come between husband and wife.

This was probably a gradual process. It may have been difficult to detect it happening. It could have begun with Isaac or Rebekah.

Perhaps Rebekah was so focused on Jacob, the child of promise ("one people will be stronger than the other, and the older will serve the younger"), that he became her favorite. Perhaps Isaac felt crowded out. He no longer strutted. He began favoring Esau.

Or perhaps as the boys grew, Isaac had more in common with the outdoor-loving Esau. They hunted and fished together. Rebekah tried to make it up to Jacob, and she overcompensated. I can imagine her late-night talks with Isaac. "You must spend more time with Jacob. You are damaging his self-esteem. You are insensitive and unfair in the way you treat him." Rebekah submitted on the outside but seethed on the inside. And Isaac's shoulders drooped a little more.

However it happened, the delightful oneness of this marriage was cracking.

Caution Signal #2

> *Now there was a famine in the land—besides the earlier famine of Abraham's time—and Isaac went to Abimelech king of the Philistines. . . . When the men of that place asked him about his wife, he said, "She is my sister," because he was afraid to say, "She is my wife." He thought, "The men of this place might kill me on account of Rebekah, because she is beautiful."*
>
> *— Genesis 26:1, 7*

One day the king of the Philistines saw Isaac caressing Rebekah. He confronted Isaac, "She is really your wife! Why did you say, 'She is my sister?'"

Isaac responded, "Because I thought I might lose my life on account of her."

The king said, "What is this you have done to us? One of the men might well have slept with your wife, and you would have brought guilt upon us." Then he ordered the people, "Anyone who molests this man or his wife shall surely be put to death" (Genesis 26:8-11).

Rebekah's disappointment that her protector put her in such an unprotected situation must have been crushing. Perhaps she never forgave him for this violation. Perhaps she never again fully entrusted herself to him. Their oneness was shattered. Submission was a huge issue. There was every reason to rationalize her way out of it.

Isaac seldom strutted anymore. He was painfully aware that his wife did not respect him. Without her respect, love, acceptance, and encouragement there was little comfort in his tent.

The reality is, every woman who submits to the authority and protection of her husband and/or to the elders of her church will be disappointed to some degree. Whether it is a minor infraction such as forgetting an anniversary or a major offense such as unfaithfulness, every husband will disappoint every wife. Whether it is elders who schedule a missions conference on the same weekend that the women have a retreat planned (which the elders approved), or elders who are insensitive to wounded women in the congregation, all elders will fail women. The explanation is simple: they are sinners.

The solution hinges on us recognizing the same thing about ourselves. We are sinners. But as redeemed sinners, we are called to reflect our redemption by forgiving. We are called to activate the redemption principle and release those indebted to us and even "supply him liberally from your flock, your threshing floor and your winepress. Give to him as the Lord your God has blessed you. Remember that you were slaves in Egypt and the Lord your God redeemed you. That is why I give you this command today" (Deuteronomy 15:12-15).

Isaac faltered, but Rebekah was not excused from her responsibility to submit. This does not mean she was to submit to sin. It does not mean that she was to be brain-dead, nor was she to be emotion-dead. It does mean that she was to forgive, and that requires enormous brain- and emotion-power. Submission means actively and voluntarily choosing to reflect my redemption in my marriage when it is easy and when it is not, when my husband deserves it and when he does not, because I was a slave in Egypt and the Lord my God redeemed me.

What if Rebekah had used this opportunity to help her husband become a stronger man? What if she had not submitted to his lie but had submissively challenged him? Suppose she had released her fear and anger to the Lord, repented of any wrong attitudes, asked for wisdom, and then chosen the right moment to approach Isaac and lovingly say, "I feel unprotected and vulnerable, but I am confident that you do not mean to hurt me. I want you to know that I am not angry or resentful, but I do not expect you to read my mind, so I think it is only right that I explain my feelings to you. Because I love you and have entrusted myself to you, I desperately need to be protected and valued by you."

This kind of submission would have expressed her forgiveness and would have "supplied him liberally" with the gift of her trust and respect. Their hearts would be knit together. Isaac would strut again.

No relationship can survive and thrive without forgiveness. Unforgiveness eats away at the soul and at the relationship.

Caution Signal #3

> Isaac planted crops in that land and the same year reaped a hundredfold, because the Lord blessed him. The man became rich, and his wealth continued to grow until he became very wealthy. He had so many flocks and herds and servants that the Philistines envied him.
>
> — Genesis 26:12-14

This is indeed disturbing.

If Rebekah had continued to be a Proverbs 31 woman who opened her arms to the poor and extended her hands to the needy in her community, I don't think the Philistines would have envied her husband. I think they would have revered him as the people in the Proverbs 31 woman's community revered her husband ("Her husband is respected at the city gate, where he takes his seat among the elders of the land" [Proverbs 31:23]).

Perhaps wealth caused Rebekah to become proud and independent, and submission gave way to superficiality—form without substance.

Separateness in marriage erodes a woman's capacity to cultivate community and to be a channel of compassion. Oneness with a husband cannot be replaced with children, friendships, activities, or possessions. The woman who is not bringing comfort to her tent will be hindered in comforting others.

These warning signals are not for the unbelieving woman. They are for the Christian woman. Rebekah was a woman of biblical faith. She knew the covenant promise. She knew that God had bound Himself to be the God of Abraham and his descendants.

Rebekah's story raises some penetrating questions.

REBEKAH'S QUESTIONS

How can one who knows the promise stray so far from the God who made the promise?

Did being a mother take precedence over being a wife? Did unforgiveness cause Rebekah to be bitter? Did pride over their wealth cause her to be insensitive to the needs around her? Did self-interest in protecting Jacob's position crowd out God's glory? Would her husband and children have been different if she had cultivated community in her own tent and taught her children to be channels of compassion to their neighbors? Would Rebekah have been different if Sarah had still been alive to train her to love her husband and children?

We are not asking Rebekah these questions. Rebekah is posing the questions to us.

What happened to Rebekah happens to all of us when we psychologize rather than theologize our life experiences.

Rebekah's experiences collided with her theology, and she yielded to experience. She did not view the world nor her life from a redemptive perspective. She did not think redemptively, so she did not reflect her redemption. She believed the covenant promise, but she waffled on God's sovereign power to keep His promise. She foolishly thought she had to help God achieve His purpose. Her zeal for God's will shifted to scheming and manipulating to bring it about. She no longer extended her hands; she grabbed to control everything and everyone in sight. Rebekah's submission problem was not with her husband; it was with God.

If we waver on submission, every other virtue crumbles.

The only way we can keep our hands and hearts open and extended is to continually go to the cross. There we see the most remarkable picture of One opening His arms to the poor and extending His hands to the needy. At the cross we see the pattern, and at the empty tomb we get the power.

Do nothing out of selfish ambition or vain conceit, but in humility consider others better than yourselves. Each of you should look not only to your own interests, but also to the interests of others. Your attitude should be the same as that of Christ Jesus: Who, being in very nature God, did not consider equality with God something to be grasped, but made himself nothing, taking the very nature of a servant, being made in human likeness. And being found in appearance as a man, he humbled himself and became obedient to death—even death on a cross! Therefore God exalted him to the highest place and gave him the name that is above every name, that at the name of Jesus every knee should bow, in heaven and on earth and under the earth, and every tongue confess that Jesus Christ is Lord, to the glory of God the Father.

— *Philippians 2:3-11*

I cannot give logical arguments for submission. It defies logic that Jesus would release all the glories of heaven so He could give *us* the glory of heaven. Submission is not about logic; it is about love.

Jesus loved us so much that He voluntarily submitted to death on a cross. His command is that wives are to submit to their husbands. It is a gift that we voluntarily give to the man we have vowed to love in obedience to the Savior we love.

THE CHALLENGE

In her novel *Stepping Heavenward*, Elizabeth Prentiss gives a clever comparison of subservience and submission. In the story, the main character, Katy, writes her thoughts in her journal. This particular entry is about her sister-in-law, Martha, who lives with Katy and Ernest.

Today Martha has a house-cleaning mania, and has dragged me into it by representing the sin and misery of those deluded mortals who think servants know how to sweep and to scrub. In spite of my resolution not to get under her thumb,

I have somehow let her rule and reign over me to such an extent that I can hardly sit up long enough to write this. Does the whole duty of woman consist in keeping her house distressingly clean and prim; in making and baking and preserving and pickling; in climbing to the top shelves of closets lest perhaps a little dust should lodge there, and getting down on her hands and knees to inspect the carpet?

The truth is there is not one point of sympathy between Martha and myself, not one. One would think that our love to Ernest would furnish it. But her love aims at the abasement of his character and mine at its elevation. She thinks I should bow down to and worship him, jump up and offer him my chair when he comes in, feed him with every unwholesome dainty he fancies, and feel myself honored by his acceptance of these services. I think it is for him to rise and offer me a seat, because I am a woman and his wife; and that a silly subservience on my part is degrading to him and to myself. And I am afraid I make known these sentiments to her in a most unpalatable way.[3]

This commentary shatters the notion that the true woman's perspective on submission is synonymous with mindless passivity or manipulative smothering. Submission is not silly subservience that degrades men or women. Our challenge is to pray for wisdom to understand, respect, and appreciate our husbands' maleness so that our submission elevates his character.

In *Male and Female Realities*, Joe Tanenbaum gives some interesting observations about male/female relationships. Even though his presuppositions and definitions are not Christian, some of his research is helpful. He says that it takes an immense amount of energy for men to venture from the physical/intellectual plane into an emotional or spiritual one; it's exhausting and therefore threatening to them. It makes men feel far more vulnerable than most women could ever possibly understand. He suggests that just as men must take care not to overpower women physically, women must be careful not to overpower men on an emotional level. Neither kind of power play is right.

Because Tanenbaum believes that men are rooted in the concrete/physical mode, he claims they tend to convert the spiritual dimension of life into physical forms. "When a religious man talks about his religion, he usually talks about its principles, structure, rituals, history, and celebrations. . . . A man finds comfort in rules and regulations [of the faith] so that he does not have to venture into the [more nebulous] spiritual realm very often."[4]

Obviously Tanenbaum is not taking into account the supernatural work of the Holy Spirit and the transforming power of the Gospel. But his observations can help us to understand, appreciate, and accommodate male/female differences. His account of a man in one of his workshops can help us approach submission with greater wisdom. In this example, Tanenbaum relates that the man talked about how he always felt unsure of his relationship with his wife.

> He loved her and wanted to be with her for the rest of his life, but he felt a sense of uneasiness that he couldn't put his finger on. After struggling with this realization for a few minutes, he began to cry. . . . When we pursued the question, he said he was afraid his wife would leave because he didn't understand why she was with him in the first place. He knew she loved him, but there was an intangible part of her that he felt he could never reach. A nagging little piece of his mind had him wondering about the stability of the relationship since he could not contain the "whole" of it. He knew she was "holding" the relationship, but he couldn't; and he was afraid that if she let go, the relationship would deteriorate and there would be nothing he could do about it.
>
> I was surprised at his insight and thrilled with his openness and his direct honesty. . . . I asked the other men in the room how they felt about what had just been revealed. All the men said that they had never verbalized that feeling before, but that it was also true for them. The wives in the room were

surprised at the tenderness of their husbands and deeply appreciated the vulnerability that their husbands must have felt. The wives began to see how the husbands were viewing their relationships; how the men depended on them to maintain stability; and how much the men needed reassurances that the relationship was in good shape. I frequently use this example in men's groups, and the participants always validate the experience of uncertainty regarding their relationship and the role they play in them.

This has implications for the husband/wife relationship and for male/female relationships in the church. Countless husbands have looked incredulously at their wives when they have vented their need for "more depth in our relationship" and murmured, "I just don't understand you." He really doesn't understand, and she overpowers him emotionally by demanding that he cross into such unfamiliar territory. She throws painful emotional blows that make him feel uncertain and vulnerable. She is not building community with her husband. She is not being a channel of compassion to him. She is not submitting to his need for her to be his helper.

It is quite possible that the ordained male leadership in a church may have somewhat the same feeling about the "intangible" aspect of the faith of women. That intuitive, sensitive aspect of our femaleness often gives us a deeper understanding of body life, simply because of the way we perceive things. So we must be careful to reassure male leadership and not to run ahead of them. If women were in charge, we would tend to elevate the experiential aspects of the faith above the principles of the faith. We need men to keep giving us the concrete foundational principles, and they need us to keep reminding them of the relational practices.

I am in no way minimizing the frustration of gender differences. But the uncomfortable truth is that this frustration is a warning signal that I am not appreciating God's creation design of gender differences to bring completeness and balance to the home and church.

The true woman will be sensitive to a man's uncertainty in venturing into the emotional realm and make it a safe thing for him to do. She doesn't demand it of him or accuse him for his failure; she reaches out with acceptance and says, "This is a safe place to be." When I see a man who is comfortable listening to and learning from women, I wonder about the woman who made it safe for him. Idelette Calvin was such a woman. Following her death, her husband John Calvin wrote to his friend Pierre Viret: "My sorrow is no common one. I have lost the excellent companion of my life, who, if misfortune had come upon us, would have gladly shared with me, not merely exile in wretchedness, but death itself. . . . She has always been a faithful helper in my work. Never have I suffered the least hindrance from her."[6]

THE CELEBRATION

In the last recorded chapter on Rebekah (Genesis 27), she learns that Esau plans to kill Jacob, so she again takes control. Rather than trusting God's promise, she convinces her husband to send Jacob back to her family to get a wife. She never sees her beloved son again. There are consequences to sin.

If this were the end of the story, it would be a sad conclusion, but I do not believe this is the last chapter on Rebekah. We do not need *her* last chapter because we have *the* last chapter.

Rebekah has a Mediator who cried, as Moses did, "O God, please heal her" (Numbers 12:13). She has a Savior who promised, "Never will I leave you; never will I forsake you" (Hebrews 13:5). She has the promise that " . . . he who began a good work in you will carry it on to completion until the day of Christ Jesus" (Philippians 1:6).

The celebratory aspect of Rebekah's story is not Rebekah's triumph; it is the triumph of persevering grace. This is our hope. Our God is relentless. We are His temple, and He has declared, "I have consecrated this temple . . . by putting my Name there forever. My eyes and my heart will always be there" (1 Kings 9:3).

At one point I felt disloyal in exposing Rebekah's failures. I wondered why God did not give us another chapter that told of her repentance, of reconciliation with her husband and children, and of this family living happily ever after. Then I realized God did write that chapter. The whole of Scripture is that chapter. "Ever after" is eternity. I could almost hear Rebekah shouting, "Write my small story so other women will hear the grand story of redemption. Write about my failures so other women will learn how 'to love their husbands and children . . . so that no one will malign the word of God'" (Titus 2:4-5).

As you and I learn from Rebekah, God redeems her failures and transforms them into treasures. He does the same with my failures. His grace is inexhaustible.

IN SUMMARY

God said that man needs a helper. The true woman celebrates this calling and becomes affirming rather than adversarial, compassionate rather than controlling, a partner rather than a protagonist. She becomes substantively rather than superficially submissive.

The true woman is not afraid to place herself in a position of submission. She does not have to grasp; she does not have to control. Her fear dissolves in the light of God's covenant promise to be her God and to live within her. Submission is simply a demonstration of her confidence in the sovereign power of the Lord God. Submission is a reflection of her redemption.

The true woman "opens her arms to the poor and extends her hands to the needy" (Proverbs 31:20) with freedom and beauty because she has submitted to her husband and to the ordained male leadership in her church.

Personal Reflection

1. If you're married, which stage of Rebekah's marriage describes your marriage?

2. Have you been disappointed by a man in authority over you? Have you forgiven him?

3. Ask God to search your heart and to show you any sinful attitudes toward the men in your life.

4. Make a commitment to pray for the men in your life. Don't give God a list of ways to change them. Rather, select a Scripture such as Philippians 1:3-6 or Colossians 1:9-12 and pray this for them. Write your commitment in your journal.

5. Now that we have come to the conclusion of this study, what is your reaction to the true-woman concept? List three things that you have learned from this study that have been helpful to you.

6. Write a statement of your life purpose and a statement of your worldview. Then compare your statements with the ones you wrote in chapter 2.

7. How do you define yourself? After writing your answer, compare it with the answer you wrote in chapter 3.

CONCLUSION

*I shall never wonder at anything that female fortitude,
when upheld by Divine grace, can do, after it could stand
in the person of Mary, at the foot of the cross, when
Christ her Son and her Lord was suspended upon it.*

Female Piety

The hotel lobby was filled with teenagers. I was there for a women's conference; they were there for a prom. I particularly noticed the girls. Their sequined dresses sparkled. But when I looked at their faces, there was no sparkle. Rather than fresh innocence, I saw hardened boredom. I frantically searched the crowd for one face that radiated piety and purity. My mind raced back to my visit with Rosalie Cassels. At eighty she reflects more radiance than these eighteen-year-old girls. My heart wept.

In the beginning of this book, I said that my prayer was that you would be captivated by the concept of the true woman and stirred to be one. It will take enormous female fortitude to be a true woman, but by God's Word and Spirit we can do it. We must do it. We must show the girls in our families, churches, neighborhoods, and communities a true reflection of womanhood.

The true woman is one whose redeemed character is being shaped and driven by God's Word. She is a true reflection of God's glory. This is not just a tall order—it is a terrifying order. We live in a culture that does not value our value system. Our culture is not just complacent toward true womanhood—there is an ever-expanding hostility toward piety, purity, domesticity, and submission. The only thing powerful enough to assuage our terror and their hostility is God's glory. As we live in the presence of His glory, we can courageously face the world and radiate His glory.

I would be less than honest if I did not warn you that your decision to reflect your redemption will be resisted. So in conclusion I would like to give you a letter to read when you meet that resistance. Whether the opposition is from within (a personal sin struggle) or without, I pray that this letter will encourage you.

Dear Sister,

I know this is a difficult time. Since I can't put my arms around you and weep with you, let me share some thoughts that have helped me walk paths of pain with a pilgrim perspective of the world and of my life.

" . . . Since we are surrounded by such a great cloud of witnesses, let us throw off everything that hinders and the sin that so easily entangles, and let us run with perseverance the race marked out for us. Let us fix our eyes on Jesus, the author and perfecter of our faith, who for the joy set before him endured the cross, scorning its shame, and sat down at the right hand of the throne of God. Consider him who endured such opposition from sinful men, so that you will not grow weary and lose heart" (Hebrews 12:1-3).

As you run this uphill portion of your life race, remember that it has been marked out for you by our sovereign God. This hill did not catch Him by surprise. Run your race deliberately and carefully. Think about those true women who have finished with honors and are cheering you on. Think about Mary Fish, Elizabeth Prentiss, Mary, Miriam, Rahab, Dorcas, and Rebekah. Throw off every doubt and fear that can entangle you. Disentangle from the impulses to manipulate and control your situation. Do not allow yourself to get tripped up thinking about who did what, who didn't do what, what's going to happen. Fix your eyes on Jesus. His joy was not the race but the crown beyond the cross. Meditate on Him so that you will not grow weary and lose heart.

You probably feel that you are being shaken to the very core, and that may be exactly what is happening. Paul records the promise from heaven: "'Once more I will shake not only the earth but also the heavens.' The words 'once more' indicate the removing of what can be shaken—that is, created things—so that what cannot be shaken may remain. Therefore, since we are receiving a kingdom that cannot be shaken, let us be thankful, and so worship God acceptably with reverence and awe, for our 'God is a consuming fire'" (Hebrews 12:26-29).

As I view the lives of women who have reflected their redemption through disappointments and difficulties, I realize that so much has been shaken off from them that I see a clearer reflection of Jesus in them. Think about the women whose stories are recorded in this book. God has removed what can be shaken from them, and what cannot be shaken remains. Self has been shaken away. Jesus shines through.

"Those who trust in the Lord are like Mount Zion, which cannot be shaken but endures forever. As the mountains surround Jerusalem, so the Lord surrounds his people both now and forevermore" (Psalm 125:1-2).

This is a battle, but it is not about what is happening to you. This is about redemption. This is your moment to reflect your redemption. Be a true woman. Give a true reflection of your Redeemer. "And we, who with unveiled faces all reflect the Lord's glory, are being transformed into his likeness with ever-increasing glory, which comes from the Lord, who is the Spirit" (2 Corinthians 3:18).

You are being transformed into His likeness, and it is beautiful to behold.

With much love and many prayers,

ABOUT THE AUTHOR

S usan Hunt is a pastor's wife. She and her husband, Gene, have three adult children and six grandchildren. She currently serves as Women in the Church Consultant for the Presbyterian Church in America's Christian Education Committee. She has degrees from the University of South Carolina and Columbia Theological Seminary.

This is Susan's fifth book. Her other books include:

Spiritual Mothering: The Titus 2 Model for Women Mentoring Women.

Leadership for Women in the Church, co-authored with Peggy Hutcheson.

By Design: God's Distinctive Calling for Women.

ABC Bible Verses for Children.

Susan may be contacted through the Christian Education office of the Presbyterian Church in America at 1852 Century Place, Suite 101, Atlanta, GA 30345, phone (404) 320-3388.

$\mathcal{N}$ OTES

PART ONE
THE TRUE WOMAN VERSUS THE NEW WOMAN

Chapter One
Her Time

1. Alexis de Tocqueville, *Democracy in America*, vol. 2 (New York: Alfred A. Knopf, 1945; Vintage Books, a division of Random House, 1990), 198.

2. John Angell James, *Female Piety* (London: Hamilton Adams and Company, 1860; reprint, Pittsburgh: Soli Deo Gloria Publications—P. O. Box 451, Morgan, Penn., 15064, FAX 412/221-1902—1994), 72.

3. W. E. Vine, *An Expository Dictionary of New Testament Words*, vol. 4 (Old Tappan, N.J.: Fleming H. Revell, 1966), 158.

4. Barbara Welter, "The Cult of True Womanhood: 1820-1860," *American Quarterly*, 18 (Summer 1966), 151.

5. David F. Wells, *No Place for Truth* (Grand Rapids: Eerdmans, 1993), 26-27.

6. Welter, "Cult of True Womanhood," 152.

7. Ibid., 174.

8. James, *Female Piety*, 72.

9. Welter, "Cult of True Womanhood," 153.

10. Tocqueville, *Democracy in America*, 214.

11. *The Presbyterian Layman*, 27, no. 1, (January/February 1994).

12. *Focus on the Family Newsletter*, Colorado Springs, Colo., October 1995.

13. Peggy Noonan, "You'd Cry Too if it Happened to You," *Forbes*, September 14, 1992, 60, 64, 65, 69.

14. Ibid.

15. Ibid.

16. Wells, *No Place for Truth*, 293-94.

17. James, *Female Piety*, 73.

Chapter Two
Her Standard

1. *The Westminster Confession of Faith, Together with the Larger Catechism and the Shorter Catechism* (Atlanta: Presbyterian Church in America Committee for Christian Education & Publications, 1990).

2. Barbara Welter, "The Cult of True Womanhood: 1820-1860," *American Quarterly*, 18 (Summer 1966), 174.

3. J. I. Packer, *The Quest for Godliness: The Puritan Vision of the Christian Life* (Wheaton, Ill.: Crossway Books, 1990), 22.

4. *The Origin and Formation of The Westminster Confession of Faith, an Article in The Westminster Confession of Faith* (Atlanta: Presbyterian Church in America Committee for Christian Education & Publications, 1990).

5. Ibid., 5.

6. Ibid., Catechism Question 3.

7. Joy Day Buel and Richard Buel, Jr., *The Way of Duty: A Woman and Her Family in Revolutionary America* (New York: W. W. Norton & Company, 1984), xi-xiii.

8. Ibid., 7-8.

9. Ibid., 89.

10. Ibid., 105.

11. Ibid., 121.

12. Ibid., 253.

13. Ibid., 280.

14. Ibid., 230.

15. Ibid., 281.

16. George Lewis Prentiss, *More Love to Thee: The Life & Letters of Elizabeth Prentiss* (Amityville, N.Y.: Calvary Press, 1994), 1. This edition is a photolithograph of the 1882 edition by A. D. F. Randolph, New York.

17. Elizabeth Prentiss, *Stepping Heavenward* (Amityville, N.Y.: Calvary Press, 1993), Editor's Preface. This is a reprint from A. D. F. Randolph's 1880 edition, New York.

18. Prentiss, *More Love to Thee*, 372.

19. Ibid., 298.

20. Ibid., 411.

21. Alexis de Tocqueville, *Democracy in America*, vol. 2 (New York: Alfred A. Knopf, 1945; Vintage Books, a division of Random House, 1990), 213-14.

22. David F. Wells, *No Place for Truth* (Grand Rapids: Eerdmans, 1993), 31-32.

23. Ibid., 95.

24. Tocqueville, *Democracy in America*, 201-02.

25. Ibid., 203.

PART TWO
HER IDENTITY

Chapter Three
A Recipient of Redemption

1. John Angell James, *Female Piety* (London: Hamilton Adams and Company, 1860; reprint, Pittsburgh: Soli Deo Gloria Publications, 1994), 22-23.

2. George Grant, *The Micah Mandate* (Chicago: Moody Press, 1995), 80.

3. John Murray, *Redemption Accomplished and Applied* (Grand Rapids: Wm. B. Eerdmans Publishing Company, 1955), Preface.

4. R. C. Sproul, "A Man for All Seasons," *Tabletalk*, Ligonier Ministries, October 1995, 6.

5. John Calvin, *Calvin's Institutes of the Christian Religion*, vol. 1 (Philadelphia: The Westminster Press, 1960), 38.

6. *The Westminster Confession of Faith, Together with the Larger Catechism and the Shorter Catechism* (Atlanta: Presbyterian Church in America Committee for Christian Education & Publications, 1990). Shorter Catechism, Question 11.

7. Calvin, *Calvin's Institutes*, 202.

8. Ibid, 220.

9. Ibid, 298.

10. Quoted in *Tabletalk*, November 1992, 13-14.

11. Paul Kooistra, "President's Report," Covenant Theological Seminary, 1993.

12. Murray, *Redemption Accomplished*, 42-43.

13. Oswald Chambers, *My Utmost for His Highest* (New York: Dodd, Mead & Co., 1959), November 26.

14. Murray, *Redemption Accomplished*, 77-78.

Chapter Four
A Reflection of Redemption

1. *The Westminster Confession of Faith, Together with the Larger Catechism and the Shorter Catechism* (Atlanta: Presbyterian Church in America Committee for Christian Education & Publications, 1990), Westminster Shorter Catechism, Question 35.

2. George Grant, *The Micah Mandate* (Chicago: Moody Press, 1995), 15.

3. George Lewis Prentiss, *More Love to Thee: The Life & Letters of Elizabeth Prentiss* (Amityville, N.Y.: Calvary Press, 1994), 411.

4. Westminster Shorter Catechism, Question 87.

5. R. Laird Harris, Gleason L. Archer, Jr., Bruce K. Waltke, *Theological Wordbook of the Old Testament* (Chicago: Moody Press, 1980), 80.

6. Ibid., 132.

7. Prentiss, *More Love to Thee*, 366.

8. Ibid., 367-68.

9. Oswald Chambers, *My Utmost for His Highest* (New York: Dodd, Mead & Co., 1959), January 7.

Chapter Five
A Cultivator of Community

1. *The Westminster Confession of Faith, Together with the Larger Catechism and the Shorter Catechism* (Atlanta: Presbyterian Church in America Committee for Christian Education and Publications, 1990), Westminster Confession of Faith, XXVI, 1.

2. Ibid., XXVI, 2.

3. Cited in Peter Marshall and David Manuel, *The Light and the Glory* (Old Tappan, N.J.: Fleming H. Revell Co., 1977), 162.

4. R. Laird Harris, Gleason L. Archer, Jr., Bruce K. Waltke, *Theological Wordbook of the Old Testament* (Chicago: Moody Press, 1980), 661.

5. George Grant, *The Micah Mandate* (Chicago: Moody Press, 1995), 219-20.

6. George Lewis Prentiss, *More Love to Thee: The Life & Letters of Elizabeth Prentiss* (Amityville, N.Y.: Calvary Press, 1994), 370.

Chapter Six
A Channel of Compassion

1. John Angell James, *Female Piety* (London: Hamilton Adams and Company, 1860; reprint, Pittsburgh: Soli Deo Gloria Publications, 1994), 251.

2. P. H. Gwinn, "A Remarkable Christian Woman," *Christian Observer*, Manassas, Va., September 9, 1903.

3. *The Westminster Confession of Faith, Together with the Larger Catechism and the Shorter Catechism* (Atlanta: Presbyterian Church in America Committee for Christian Education & Publications, 1990), Westminster Shorter Catechism, Question 87.

4. *The Catechism for Young Children* (Atlanta: Presbyterian Church in America, Committee for Christian Education and Publications), Question 56.

PART THREE
HER VIRTUE

Chapter Seven
Piety

1. William J. Bennett, *The Book of Virtues* (New York: Simon & Schuster, 1993), 11-12.

2. Oswald Chambers, *My Utmost for His Highest* (New York: Dodd, Mead & Co., 1959), December 30.

3. John Calvin, *Calvin's Institutes of the Christian Religion*, vol. 1 (Philadelphia: The Westminster Press, 1960), 40-41.

4. J. I. Packer, *The Quest for Godliness: The Puritan Vision of the Christian Life* (Wheaton, Ill.: Crossway Books, 1990), 331.

5. Ibid., 332.

6. Alexis de Tocqueville, *Democracy in America*, vol. 2 (New York: Alfred A. Knopf, 1945; Vintage Books, a division of Random House, 1990), 211.

7. John Angell James, *Female Piety* (London: Hamilton Adams and Company, 1860; reprint, Pittsburgh: Soli Deo Gloria Publications, 1994), 133.

8. George Lewis Prentiss, *More Love to Thee: The Life & Letters of Elizabeth Prentiss* (Amityville, N.Y.: Calvary Press, 1994), 26.

9. Ibid., 35.

10. Ibid., 374.

11. Ibid., 406.

12. *The Westminster Confession of Faith, Together with the Larger Catechism and the*

Shorter Catechism (Atlanta: Presbyterian Church in America Committee for Christian Education & Publications, 1990), Westminster Shorter Catechism, Question 35.

13. Packer, Quest for Godliness, 24.

Chapter Eight
Purity

1. R. Laird Harris, Gleason L. Archer, Jr., Bruce K. Waltke, Theological Wordbook of the Old Testament, vol. 1 (Chicago: Moody Press, 1980), 344.

2. The Westminster Confession of Faith, Together with the Larger Catechism and the Shorter Catechism (Atlanta: Presbyterian Church in America Committee for Christian Education & Publications, 1990), Westminster Shorter Catechism, Question 33.

3. R. C. Sproul, general ed., "'This Is My Name': God's Self-Disclosure," New Geneva Study Bible (Nashville: Thomas Nelson, 1995), p. 98.

4. Harris, Archer, Waltke, Theological Wordbook, 682.

5. S. G. DeGraaf, Promise and Deliverance, vol. 1 (St. Catherine's, Ontario: Paideia Press, 1977), 340.

Chapter Nine
Domesticity

1. John Angell James, Female Piety (London: Hamilton Adams and Company, 1860; reprint, Pittsburgh: Soli Deo Gloria Publications, 1994), 75.

2. Ibid., 92.

3. George Grant, "Victoria's Secret: Bad Ideas Don't Last," Tabletalk, vol. 20, no. 2, Ligonier Ministries, February 1996, 58-59.

4. J. I. Packer, The Quest for Godliness: The Puritan Vision of the Christian Life (Wheaton, Ill.: Crossway Books, 1990), 272-73.

5. James, Female Piety, 377.

Chapter Ten
Submission

1. Susan Hunt, By Design (Franklin, Tenn: Legacy Communications, 1994), 34.

2. Edna Gerstner, Jonathan and Sarah: An Uncommon Union (Pittsburgh, Pa.: Soli Deo Gloria Publications, 1995), 205.

3. Elizabeth Prentiss, Stepping Heavenward (Amityville, N.Y.: Calvary Press, 1993, reprinted from A. D. F. Randolph and Company's 1880 edition), 118.

4. Joe Tanenbaum, *Male and Female Realities* (San Marcos, Calif.: Robert Erdmann, 1990), 65.

5. Ibid., 175.

6. Edna Gerstner, *Idelette* (Pittsburgh, Pa.: Soli Deo Gloria Publications, 1995), 160.